SURBITON BOMBED

SURBITON, Tolworth and Berrylands suffered badly in the Second World War. At least 400 bombs rained down on the Surbiton borough, many of which demolished family homes, shops, offices and roads. Fifty-nine innocent victims lost their lives. And while memorial services often remember those who perished in the battlefields or were shot out of the skies above, there has been, up to now, little mention of those civilians whose often young lives were cut cruelly short at home. Here, we recall their names and study, for the first time, a full volume of striking and contemporary photographs 'captured' on camera to record the results of the enemy's raids. For years, these priceless black and white pictures taken by Surbiton Council were out of the public eye — at first because of Government restrictions on their publication and later because they were in storage. Now, this wonderful collection, archived at Kingston Museum's History Centre, has been published here as a set together with many stories and extra illustrations from those who lived through the war years. For many people the dramatic images will bring back poignant memories — of sadness, hardship and pain, but also that warm feeling of togetherness and neighbourliness which enabled many residents to survive such a dark period in our history.

ON 3rd SEPTEMBER 1939, families in Surbiton and Tolworth, along with those all over the land, listened to the Prime Minister, Neville Chamberlain, making an announcement on the wirelss at 11 o'clock saying that war had begun between Britain and Germany.

This sketch, by Doreen Conroy, nee Wells, of Tolworth, depicts that day in her parents' home in Douglas Road, Tolworth, when she was just 10 years old. The wireless, powered by a battery accumulator, brings the news into the front room of the family home at No 23.

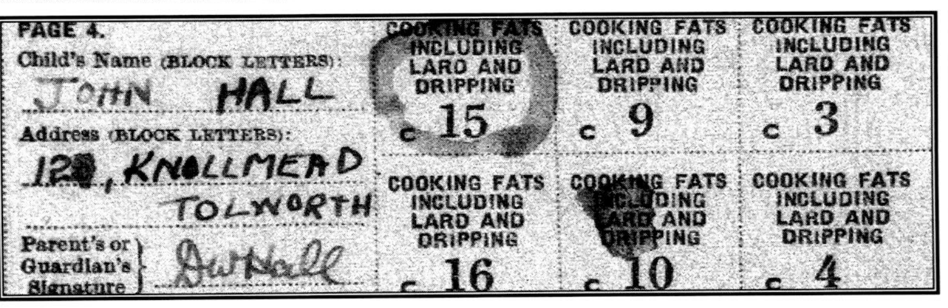
PAGE 4.
Child's Name (BLOCK LETTERS): JOHN HALL
Address (BLOCK LETTERS): 12?, KNOLLMEAD TOLWORTH
Parent's or Guardian's Signature: [illegible]

COOKING FATS INCLUDING LARD AND DRIPPING c 15	COOKING FATS INCLUDING LARD AND DRIPPING c 9	COOKING FATS INCLUDING LARD AND DRIPPING c 3
COOKING FATS INCLUDING LARD AND DRIPPING c 16	COOKING FATS INCLUDING LARD AND DRIPPING c 10	COOKING FATS INCLUDING LARD AND DRIPPING c 4

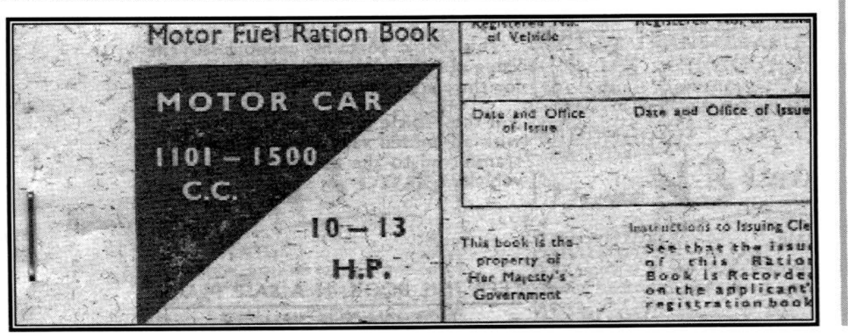
Motor Fuel Ration Book
MOTOR CAR
1101 – 1500 C.C.
10 – 13 H.P.
Date and Office of Issue
Date and Office of Issue
This book is the property of Her Majesty's Government

Acknowledgments

Jill Lamb and Emma Rummins, Kingston Museum and Heritage Service; Trevor Archer; Eric Heather; Eileen Stone; Doreen Conroy; Joyce Borup, Irene Kearsey, Dorothy Hall, John Hall, Ray Hart; David Wood; Muriel Davison; Gladys Millard; June Phillips; Eileen Pepperell; Peter and Joyce Lewis and family; Ray Lloyd; Betty Miller, David Tippett-Wilson; Ray Stacey; Joyce and Eddie Gardener; Jill Adams; Ray Austin, Chris Patey and numerous kind readers of the *Remembered* series of books who have written in with various anecdotes to share with others.

Photograph credits

Kingston Museum and Heritage Service and the many people mentioned in the acknowledgements above who have supplied pictures from their family albums. Legal and General; John Clifford's collection; Battle of Britain Mk II, edited by Winston G. Ramsey (1980);

Bibliography

Surrey at War, by Bob Ogley; Surbiton Past, by Richard Statham; Germany's Secret Weapons in World War II, by Roger Ford; Put That Light Out! by Mike Brown; The Battle of Britain by Richard Hough and Denis Richards; Archives in Kingston History Centre; Surrey Comet; Air Raid Wardens' diary.

Front cover photograph: Devastation in Villiers Close, Surbiton, on 27th December 1940

Back cover photograph: VE day party at Ladywood Road, Tolworth, 1945. Courtesy of Eileen Stone

ISBN 0-9543759-0-4

Reprinted November 2007
and February 2021

Published by Mark Davison, North Bank, Smoke Lane, Reigate, Surrey, RH2 7HJ.

Tel: 01737 221215

e-mail: mark.davison1@virgin.net

Printed by The New Ink Printing Company Ltd, Caterham.

Special thanks

Dorothy Hall, nee Lewis (born 1909).

Doreen Conroy, nee Wells.

A total of 1,704 air raid warnings sounded

How Surbiton suffered

THE first air raid on the former borough of Surbiton, which took in Tolworth, Berrylands, Hook and Chessington, took place on the night of 26-27th August 1940. Two high-explosive bombs were dropped on Leatherhead Road, Chessington, just south of the Fox and Hounds public house. There was slight damage to about 14 houses but no-one was killed.

The first fatal casualty occurred on 9th September 1940, when 41-year-old Elizabeth Loveridge was trapped in her bombed house in Elmbridge Avenue. Eight others were seriously injured in that raid which caused much damage to houses along the Kingston bypass, in Knollmead, Warren Drive, Elgar Avenue and Beresford Avenue.

Roads in the vicinity of the main railway line, and the bypass, suffered bombing for obvious reasons, and also the Ewell Road/Douglas Road area of Tolworth. The years 1940 and 1941 saw the worst of the bombing, with a comparative time of quiet after — possibly due to Hitler concentrating much more of his attention on Russia.

A concentration of incendiary bombs dropped in early 1944, causing much damage to property, but this was far less frightening than the flying bombs — 22 in total, which fell from June to November 1944.

The last major incident to be recorded was the death of air raid warden Jabez Summers and his wife, when a flying bomb landed on their home in Ashcombe Avenue, Surbiton, in November of that year.

Altogether 1,704 air raid warnings sounded in the district during the war. A total of 228 high-explosive bombs, 700 incendiary devices, 26 oil bombs and 22 flying bombs came down with devastating results. Forty-five bombs also fell but failed to explode on impact. These were subsequently detonated or made safe by the bomb disposal squad.

Seventy-eight houses in the Surbiton borough were completely destroyed by the bombing, 149 homes were damaged beyond repair, 292 were able to be lived in but were badly damaged, 257 houses suffered serious damage and 9,898 others were affected in one way or another.

Mercifully, Surbiton did not receive any hits from the second of Hitler's secret weapons, the V2 rocket, otherwise casualties and destruction would have been much greater.

The Air Raid Precautions Act had come into force in 1938 and local authorities such as Surbiton were required to make plans for wardens, first aid measures, emergency ambulances, gas decontamination, rescue, repair and demolition services. First aid posts had to be set up, gas cleansing stations established and casualty clearing stations made ready.

Following the Czechoslovakian crisis, the prospect of war seemed more likely and trenches began to be dug in local parks. Digging began in Surbiton at the end of September 1938. Alexandra Recreation Ground's shelter trenches were started on 1st October.

A number of these trenches began to collapse before they were completed and it was fortunate that war was still a year away. In February 1939, plans were made to provide shelters for thousands of people, including Surbitonians. Initially, the town was part of the Eastern Emergency Area Civil Defence, using a communications system whereby police and wardens would report details of incidents to local centres. This would be relayed via a control centre, then to regional headquarters and then via a teleprinter to the Home Security War Room in London.

The first bomb of 1941 to explode in Berrylands was on 11th January. It went off at the rear of Nos 2 & 4 and the blast caused severe damage to both homes. No 6 Chiltern Drive suffered structural damage, too, but it was not as intense. A number of neighbouring houses escaped lightly.

Protective smother led to suffocation fear

Mum and baby in shelter

DOROTHY Hall and her husband, Bert, were two of the first people to move into Knollmead on the newly-built Sunray Estate at Tolworth. In 1937, they would watch the fields turn into building sites at the back of Dorothy's mother's house at 168 Warren Road. White posts and wires began to mark the plots and the route of the new railway line extending south from Malden to Chessington.

Bert, who met his wife-to-be while lodging at her family's home when he helped build the Kingston bypass 10 years earlier, paid a £5 deposit to secure one of the new homes in Knollmead. He was allowed £17 off their chosen house at No 120 because he intended doing all the decorating himself. The mortgage was for £425. Wallpaper for most of the rooms cost 4d a roll at that time.

The house was ready on 15th October 1938 and they moved in. They soon settled in and Dorothy carried on working at Beaumaris House in Surbiton Crescent, Surbiton, as a photographic assistant in the laboratory.

A few weeks after the outbreak of war in September 1939, their first son, John, was born on what was Registration Day – 29th September 1939. The Government had ordered everyone to be registered because of the likely disruption of war. The baby had not been named and was logged as "Baby" Hall – the name which was then carried on his registration card.

Dorothy recalled: "Mum bought a really good and comfortably padded pram. Unbelievably, the price was only 10/- and it looked new."

Reflecting on the outbreak of war some 62 years later, at the age of 93, Dorothy said: "There were not any serious air raids for the first few months of the war but on 9th September 1940, there was a time bomb dropped almost opposite our house and I was in the kitchen when it actually exploded and the eight houses were completely demolished *(in Warren Drive opposite the junction with Knollmead)*.

"There was one raid when I was down in our Anderson shelter at the bottom of our garden and 14 bombs were all around us. I remember leaning over my baby son, John, as though to protect him and after everything was quiet again, I thought I had suffocated him as he had fallen asleep during all the noise. When we went indoors, we found that the French windows had been blown open, even though we had left them locked.

Toddler John Hall mimics Churchill while reading the headlines: Hitler's Sea Blitz Begins.

MINISTRY OF FOOD

CHILD'S Ration Book

OFFICIAL PAID

CHILD'S NAME AND REGISTERED ADDRESS

Compare these details with the Child's Identity Card and report any difference to the Local Food Office

DO NOT ALTER

Surname HALL
Other Names JOHN E
Address 120 Knollmead Tolworth

ISSUED JULY 1942

NAT. REG. No. CNIR 403 4

If found return to SURBITON FOOD OFFICE

SERIAL NUMBER OF BOOK C 5 E 210571

R.B.2 (CHILD)

"Baby Hall" has become "John Hall" on his ration book, issued in July 1942.

The windows would not close properly afterwards and I was burgled as a result.

"On one air raid warning, we hurried to the shelter and John arrived wearing only one wellington boot.

"John rarely left my side during the war years and my main recollection of his early words was when he raised one finger and said: 'Hark!', then 'All clear!'

"He learnt to read during the many hours that we spent in the air raid shelter.

"There were not as many air raids inland and the war seemed to be more at sea and along the coastal areas. It was known as Hitler's Sea Blitz. That winter we had a lot of snow and John was in his element making snowballs and clearing the path.

"Then, in 1944, there was a new type of bombing. We called them flying bombs *(doodlebugs)*. They were unmanned and there was no warning. All the while that the engine could be heard, they were OK, but when the engine stopped, it fell immediately. One dropped near Sheephouse Lane School, *(New Malden)*. Mothers with young children were being evacuated and as I was pregnant as well, I was able to get evacuated to Stourport and so John and I went to stay on a farm with Dad's youngest brother, Joe, and his wife.

"John enjoyed going in the fields with some of the Land Army girls and helping them with carrot weeding. He actually earned 1/-. We were there for about six weeks and when my husband Bert came to visit us in September 1944, we went back to Tolworth with him.

"When John started at school at Sheephouse Lane, I always took him to school and he carried his gas mask.

"In May 1945, VE Day was celebrated for the cessation of the war and there were street parties out in the decorated roads. John had just developed chicken pox and could not join in the Knollmead party. He was not ill so he rode around on his tricycle."

After the war Bert worked as a scenic artist at the Shepperton studios.

Evelyn Hall and her half-brother John, pictured in Knollmead, Tolworth, on 31st July 1940 – a month before the Blitz. Six of the houses in the background, in Warren Drive, were demolished when a high-explosive bomb dropped from a German plane onto No 157 on 9th September. The Sunray estate, being close to a targeted railway line, suffered greatly in the air raids.

Damage in Warren Drive

The ruins of Nos 153-165 Warren Drive, Tolworth, after the high-explosive bomb on 9th September 1940 reduced these homes to a smouldering pile of debris.

'Baby' John Hall at Knollmead on 29th September 1940. Behind him stood the row of houses in Warren Drive which were demolished on 9th September (above and below).

Day war was announced

THE day the Second World War was declared was etched on Dorothy Hall's mind all her life. At the time she was living with her husband at their new home at No 120 Knollmead, Tolworth.

"My memory of 3rd September 1939 was of a beautiful, cloudless blue sky. It was a Sunday. When it was announced on the radio that we were at war, at about 11am, the wailing sirens sounded all round and everyone went out of doors and looked up at the sky. After the straight all-clear sound, we heard the drone of aircraft. I don't remember actually seeing the planes. They might have been too high up to see them. It was strange that when there were air raids warnings we could often hear them a long distance away before the local ones sounded."

Arteries severed running for gas mask

Drama at Elmdene

BOBBIE Edwards, a painter and decorator, nearly died when the London Blitz had started. For while diving back into his house at No 49 Elmdene on Tolworth's Sunray estate, to fetch a gas mask he had forgotten to bring with him to the air raid shelter nearby, he tripped and smashed into the French windows.

A particularly jagged shard of shattered glass sliced through his arm, severing an artery.

Bobbie and his wife had been in bed when the air raid sirens sounded, so they woke up their six year old son and daughter aged three and ushered them into the Anderson shelter in their back garden.

Then Bobbie made that fateful decision to run back to get their masks.

He stumbled and crashed through the glass. In the commotion, his wife believed he had been thrust backwards by the force of a nearby bomb blast. Whatever, blood was pouring profusely from his right wrist.

"He called for me to come quickly, so I left the children in the shelter and went to see what the noise had been about.

"When I saw his wrist, I tore up a tablecloth and put a tourniquet round his upper arm and we ran, still in our nightclothes, to the doctor's on the corner of Warren Drive and Barnsbury Crescent," Gladys recalled some 60 years later. "He phoned for the ambulance which arrived quickly and Bobbie was taken to Surbiton Hospital in Ewell Road. I was told that the tourniquet saved his life and that he would have bled to death in seven minutes as his arteries were severed.

Bobbie Edwards.

Six homes at 153, 155, 157, 159, 161 & 163 Warren Drive, Tolworth, were reduced to rubble after the 30th high-explosive bomb to fall on Surbiton wrought havoc on 9th September 1940. No-one was fatally wounded. Elmdene is just to the rear of this site.

"He was in hospital for several weeks and while he was there, a house on the Kingston bypass, on which he was working as a painter, received a direct hit by a bomb. Had it not been for this accident, he might have been killed at work."

Bobbie recovered and lived to see another 35 years. He died in 1975 and later, Gladys remarried and became Mrs Millard.

In retirement at the age of 87, in Newquay, Cornwall, she wrote: "During the war, I was cycling home from work one evening when there was a dog-fight going on between two aeroplanes overhead. As I cycled along Thornhill Road, I saw machine gun bullets hitting the pavement and I cycled like mad. My sister-in-law was looking after my daughter, Sheila, that day at her home in Largewood Avenue and when I arrived there, we looked up and for the only time in the war, I actually saw silver bombs falling in the sunshine from an aircraft. One fell near the bypass by the site of what is now Tolworth Tower. It was Tolworth Odeon in those days. A workman's hut was blown high into the tree tops. Several bombs had fallen behind the houses in Knollmead."

Later in the war, during the time of the doodlebugs, Bobbie was working at Chessington on a building site and he was up ladders with his colleagues when they heard a V1 coming. Then the engine stopped. Never had men moved so fast. The bomb went off in the next street as the men lay flat on the ground. Luckily they were unhurt.

Gladys Edwards.

The remains of Nos 153-161 Elgar Avenue, Tolworth, after they suffered direct hits from high-explosive bombs on 9th September 1940.

Damage to the tune of thousands in Elgar Avenue

No 159 Elgar Avenue was one of four properties in the street reduced to a heap of debris after high-explosive bombs fell out of the sky on 9th September 1940.

Broomfield Road

Three high-explosive bombs dropped on Broomfield Road, Tolworth, on 15th September 1940. Nos 35-39 were badly damaged by one which went off in front of No 37. Another bomb wrecked sheds after it detonated in the back garden of No 35. A third bomb fell into the garden of No 40, causing just slight damage.

Elgar Avenue was one of the many residential developments which sprang up in the early 1930s on what was acres of farmland in Tolworth and Berrylands. Some of the houses blown up by the Luftwaffe on 9th September 1940 were not more than five years old. Nos 153, 155, 159, 157 & 161 suffered appallingly from the detonation of two high-explosive bombs. Fortunately, lives were spared. The remains of the original No 153 are seen her.

Vivid recollections of night Tolworth home was demolished in September 1940

Family made homeless by Ravenscar Road air raid

BEFORE war broke out, Ravenscar Road, Tolworth, was a peaceful late Victorian street where neighbours chatted over garden fences and helped each other with errands. So it seemed inconceivable that this friendly community could have suffered so badly from air raid bombing. It was not intended to be a target, no doubt. The enemy's bombardment was aimed at the Kingston bypass, nearby railway lines and the factories lining the A3.

June Phillips, then Crocker, was eight years old when war was declared. She lived with her mother and father, Cis and Bob Crocker, and three sisters at No 17 Ravenscar Road.

The family had the ground floor of a two-storey house. Her parents' bedroom was at the front, the children's at the back. In between was a scullery, coal cupboard and kitchen-cum-living room. The toilet, like many of these old houses at the time, was outside.

June's eldest sister, Phyllis, was then 10 and her other sisters, Barbara, seven, and Elsie, nearly four. Their brother, Ron, was born in June 1940, just before the Blitz began.

When the air raid warnings sounded, the family took to the safety of an Anderson shelter outside their home. It was dug in only about 18 inches deep and there was a small bench to sit on.

On the Saturday night of 28th September 1940, the family's home was bombed and they lost all of their belongings.

Luckily, they were all in the shelter in the back garden at the time, otherwise the sisters would have been orphaned, for the bedroom where their parents and baby Ron slept caught a direct hit.

Next morning, kindly neighbour Mrs Clark, the wife of Fred Clark, at No 23, took the Crocker family into her home.

June recalled in later life: "Lots of people came to see how we were after our ordeal, including Miss Penzer, our headmistress of St Matthew's girls' school. She offered to look after Barbara and me, so we spent the day at her house. We could have stayed the night there but we wanted to be with our family."

After a few days with Mr and Mrs Clark in Ravenscar Road, the girls were given accommodation with a Mrs Bulman at No 34 Lovelace Gardens, Surbiton. Mrs Bulman ran a religious club, The Young Helpers Band, for children of all ages. She kept a "lovely" house in Lovelace Gardens and had two maids who prepared the meals and helped the youngsters get ready for school in the mornings.

"We had a very happy time there and we didn't seem to take too much notice of the raids which were occurring as usual. Sometimes Mrs Bulman used to take us to sing to the forces and to the blind.

"We stayed with Mrs Bulman until the Luftwaffe decided to drop incendiary bombs and a landmine in Lovelace Gardens near her home that night. There was quite a lot of damage. We were sleeping in the basement and all the windows were blown in but there were no injuries."

The raid was in October 1940. On several occasions during the month, the Lovelace Road and Lovelace Gardens area suffered blast damage. June recalled that she and the others had to leave in the middle of the night, carefully avoiding the hose pipes from the fire engines.

"During the Blitz, our schooling was disrupted by air raids which used to happen at any time. The sirens used to sound and all the schoolchildren would go to the surface shelter in the playground of St Matthew's School. Whilst the raids were on, we did 'cats' cradle' until the all-clear was given.

"I remember wondering many times if our home would still be in one piece and if our mum was all right after the raids. When the raids got too frequent, we used to do homework instead of attending school each day."

Surbiton Borough Council found temporary furnished accommodation for the Crockers at No 69 Queen's Drive, in the Berrylands area of Surbiton. This relieved the pressure on Mrs Clark's family.

June said: "What a posh house it was – so much bigger than we were used to. We were half afraid to touch things. As there wasn't a shelter there, we used to spend nights in the public shelter which was underground in the Alexandra Recreation Ground. Quite a few people used to gather there and we had some good times. We would forget what was going on at ground level. The adults even organised a Christmas party for the children there, complete with Santa Claus.

"We didn't settle in at Queen's Drive, so Mum and Dad decided to move back to Tolworth and live at No 16 Pyne Road whilst Mrs Jackson, the regular tenant, went to live in Wales during the war."

Some of the Crocker family outside No 17 Ravenscar Road, Tolworth, three years before the outbreak of war. They were to lose their home when it suffered a direct hit in September 1940. Cis Crocker is holding her baby daughter Elsie. In front of them, from left to right, are her other daughters, Phyllis, seven; Barbara, four, and June, five.

Bombed in 1940 and 1941

The remains of No17 Ravenscar Road, Tolworth, (right) after suffering a direct hit from a high-explosive bomb dropped by the Luftwaffe on 28th September 1940. Part of No 15 can be seen on the left, after being partly demolished by workmen to make it safe. No 19 on the right, was brought down, along with Nos 21 & 23 after further bombing on 19th March 1941. No 25 survived the blasts.

The Crocker family, made homeless by the 1940 bombing of No 17 Ravenscar Road, moved back to the street in 1942 and lived at No 25. Left to right: June, Barbara, mother Cis, Phyllis, Elsie and Ron.

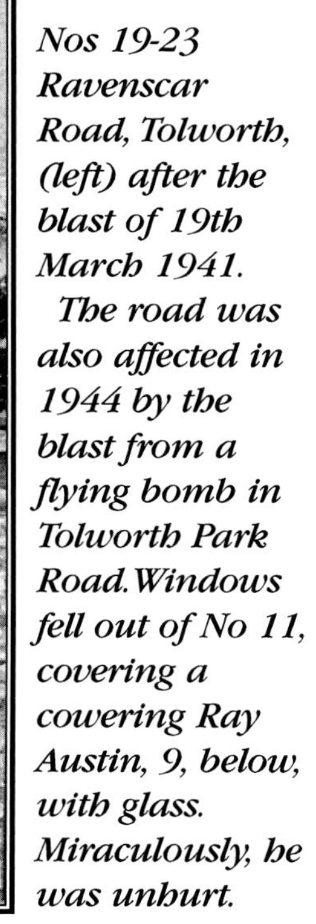

Nos 19-23 Ravenscar Road, Tolworth, (left) after the blast of 19th March 1941.

The road was also affected in 1944 by the blast from a flying bomb in Tolworth Park Road. Windows fell out of No 11, covering a cowering Ray Austin, 9, below, with glass. Miraculously, he was unhurt.

The Crocker siblings with kind neighbour Pamela Clark in 1940.

Now: The bomb site in the vicinity of No 17 Ravenscar Road redeveloped with flats.

Family disruption due to evacuation and then a return to 'dear old Tolworth'

Twice bombed out of their home in same street

THE Crocker family having been forced into temporary accommodation by the bombing of their home in Ravenscar Road, rented a house at No 16 Pyne Road, Tolworth. They continued, however, to go to the public air raid shelters at the Alexandra Recreation Ground at night, piling blankets on baby Ron's pram. This routine was eventually disrupted when bombs fell on The Fishponds, near Hollyfield Road.

In July 1941, bombs were dropped on Douglas Road causing heartbreak and devastation, especially to the Ewell Road end of Douglas Road. The explosions had flattened many buildings and there was rubble everywhere. Two small girls lost their lives. They were Jean and Barbara Strong, aged nine and five, of No 9 Douglas Road.

In that raid on 28th July, Miss Annie Hurstwaite, aged 78, of No 7 Douglas Road; Mrs Violet Archer, 41 and Ronald Archer, nine, of No 9; and Mrs Edith Trickey, 51, of 304 Ewell Road, were killed in explosions during the early hours. George Swain, 63, of Streatley, Douglas Road, died from his injuries on 8th August in Surbiton Hospital.

There had earlier been more tragedy in Ravenscar Road. On 19th March four-year-old Brenda Rising, at No 26 Ravenscar Road, was killed and Mrs Elizabeth Baigent, 41, of No 24 was fatally injured in a blast.

In April 1942, Bob Crocker was called up in the army and was eventually posted to North Africa, so his wife was left to look after the children — as many thousands of women had to at that time. By this time, the family had moved back to Ravenscar Road — to No 25.

June recalled: "How glad we were to get back to our own surroundings, even though there was now a bombed site at the side of our house, and also opposite. I recall we used to have some lovely games on our 'bombies', wandering all over what used to be people's gardens and concrete areas where the houses used to be."

In 1942, June started attending Tolworth Central School for Girls. Although the boys were in the same building, they were kept separate. The girls were upstairs and the boys down. There were also different play areas.

"Our air-raid shelters were situated along the playing fields.

"I recall a number of images: Always having to carry a gas mask; no sweets in the shops; and very little food as it was rationed. All the metal railings and gates were taken down to make into arms for the forces, we were told. We had to 'make do and mend' as clothing was only available with coupons. There were no street lights on at night; cycle lamps and torches had to be shaded; no house lights were allowed to show in the dark; and all windows were criss-crossed with strips of brown, sticky paper for safety in case of shattering in bomb blasts."

On moving back to Ravenscar Road, Bob Crocker built a fairly sophisticated shelter in the garden of No 25. It was dug in about three feet, with the help of others. It was cemented in at the bottom and sides so the children could sleep quite comfortably on mattresses. There was a bunk to one side on which Barbara slept when the raids went on all night. Candles were used for lighting. On the front of the shelter, Bob had built a lean-to so that the door to the shelter was protected from wind and rain. In the front of the shelter, Mr Crocker grew some fine lilies. On the top of the structure was a thickness of earth sufficient to grow cucumbers and marrows.

"We used to sleep in our shelter in the back garden while Dad was away. It saved us getting up in the middle of the night when the sirens sounded," June remembered. "During the raids, which were sometimes quite bad and long-lasting, I recall the whistle of the bombs falling from the bombers overhead, the gunfire from the anti-aircraft and pom-pom guns situated somewhere in the vicinity, trying to hit their targets when shown up in the beams of the searchlights.

"I recall sitting in the shelter with my fingers in my ears, trying to block out the frightening sounds. The neighbours used to come to our shelter wrapped in their coats and blankets in the night, to spend the time with us.

"In the mornings, after the raids, we used to hunt for pieces of shrapnel and compare our finds. We used to watch squadrons of bombers and fighters going out on raids day and night, counting them and checking how many were missing on return. We used to watch the Spitfires and Hurricanes doing victory rolls in the direction of the allotments at the back of our houses.

"We had to carry our gasmasks wherever we went. They had to be checked every so often at school and also a place in Surbiton. We also had identity cards to carry. We made fabric cases for them in our needlework lesson at St Matthew's School. In the year 2002, at her retirement home in Kingston, June still possessed that case as a memento of the period.

Cis Crocker with two of her children, Elsie and Ron at neighbouring No 23 Ravenscar Road, Tolworth, in 1940. Twice they were bombed out of their homes in the road.

"After the Blitz in London, Hitler sent the V1 flying bomb — or doodlebug as it was usually called. We used to listen for this engine making a grating sound, then it would cut out and we would wait for the big bang. After the explosion, we used to get out of the shelter to look for the smoke and clouds of dust on the skyline to see where it had dropped.

"I also remember that on Derby Day in 1944 we were listening to the wireless when we heard a plane, but thought it was one of ours. Mum was just opening the back door to make sure when there was this almighty explosion. The back door fell in on Mum and the wireless, which was on the table by the window, fell to the ground. The cloth on which it stood went over Barbara's head. She had been sitting beside the table. The window frame came away from the wall but didn't fall. It just stayed in a crazy position.

"I shot under the table and I think Elsie followed suit. Phyllis grabbed Ron. There was dust everywhere, the ceiling was drooping but luckily it didn't come down on us. A large crack appeared in the wall separating the kitchen and the front room. We went outside and discovered that a doodlebug had dropped in the direction of Tolworth Park Road and we had caught the blast.

"All our windows were smashed, all the ceilings in the bedroom and front room had fallen down, leaving our home in quite a state.

"Once again, we had to find refuge and my Uncle Bill and Aunty May kindly took us into their home in Douglas Road. My mum and brother Ron had to go to the first air post at the Church Hall as they had been cut by flying glass.

"We stayed at Uncle Bill's until our house could be restored to order again. It took me a long time before I ventured upstairs to the bedrooms. I was afraid they might collapse after all the damage."

Eventually, the Crockers decided to be evacuated and were taken to Winterslow in Wiltshire, but only stayed there five days. They did not like being split up.

"Mum and Ron were in one home. Barbara and Elsie were in another. Phyllis and I were in yet a different place. We were so glad to get back to dear old Tolworth — bombs and all.

"When Dad was demobbed, we hung a tea towel with the words "Welcome Home Dad" on it at the front door, but Dad didn't see it. He chose to come around the back way. Ron, who hadn't seen much of his dad in his young life, asked Mum: 'What do I call him?' and remarked how small his father was."

Brenda Rising aged four, and Mrs Elizabeth Baigent were fatally wounded when Nos 24 and 26 Ravenscar Road, Tolworth, took a direct hit from a bomb on 19th March 1941. The Crocker family lived opposite.

No 25 Ravenscar Road today.

Ravenscar Road had a tight-knit community which rallied together in times of crisis.

June Phillips can recall many of the names of the families living there in that period. They include: Sawyer, Smallpiece, Prothero, Pugh, Austin, Spratling, Millis, Allen, Ebdon, Stride, Clark, Corps, Mercer, Todd, Armor, Webb, Aldridge, Deacon, Anspach, Sims, Knight, Drake, Parsons, Elwood, Paterson, Wilson, Stone, Mortimer, Baigent, Boots, Greenslade, Midmore and Hamlet.

Cyril Cheshire of No 64 Ravenscar Road was the neighbourhood's air raid warden. He used to patrol the streets on his scooter and give residents the all-clear or not, depending on whether a raid was imminent.

Residents bought their groceries from Bourne's shop and their bread from Mogford's, the baker's. Families purchased halfpenny rolls for breakfast early in the morning which were still hot from the ovens.

In ruins: No 10 Elmbridge Avenue and neighbouring property after the bomb of 9th September 1940.

The remains of Nos 10 and 12 Elmbridge Avenue after the explosion rocked the road. The houses were barely 10 years old.

First fatality was in Elmbridge Avenue

FOR 57 consecutive days, from 7th September 1940, London and its suburbs were repeatedly bombarded — the aim being to weaken the British spirit in and around the capital.

The 12th high-explosive bomb to hit the Surbiton borough in 1940 fell on Nos 10 & 12 Elmbridge Avenue on 9th September. The two homes were demolished but remarkably there were no fatalities at these addresses. No 10 was the household of Edwin Isherwood Cobb and at No 12 resided Albert Welch.

Elizabeth Loveridge, aged 41, died from asphyxiation after being buried under rubble after the seventh high-explosive bomb to fall in the borough of Surbiton devastated Nos 64, 66 & 68 Elmbridge Avenue. The victim lived at No 66 and was the first person to lose their life in the borough as a result of enemy action on the town and its people.

No 64 was the home of Leslie Welland at the outbreak of war and Archibald Masterton resided at No 68. Other neighbours included Leonard Cope at No 60, Harry Broom at No 58 and Harold Land at No 70.

A bungalow at Elmbridge Avenue wrecked by a high-explosive bomb on 9th September 1940.

Policeman warned Surrey communist that Nazis may kill him

How Tolworth Broadway traders beat the war blues

Three years before the outbreak of the Second World War, Norman and Edith Lewis moved from Streatham to Tolworth so Norman could manage one of the new shops that had opened in The Broadway.

The shop traded as W. Clarke & Son and was a high class grocer's — one in a chain of 15 branches dotted around London.

Many people may remember the wonderful aroma that used to waft along Tolworth Broadway from the coffee roasting machine that seemed to be busy at all times of the day.

Prior to arriving in Tolworth, Norman had won an international window dressing championship organised by The Grocer magazine. Naturally, then, his window displays at Tolworth were impeccable and alluring.

During the Second World War, Norman became increasingly worried about the lack of really good warm clothing provided for Merchant Navy sailors on the highly dangerous Arctic convoys to the Soviet Union and called a meeting with as many managers of the other Broadway shops as he could. It was decided to hold a concert party called The Broadway Follies, featuring all the shopkeepers. Mostly with no acting experience at all, they practised so devotedly that they seemed to reach a standard worthy of a West End production.

Six shows were staged between 1942 and 1945 and were presented at the British Legion Hall in Hollyfield Road, Surbiton. Tickets sold like hot cakes and much-needed cash was raised for the Merchant Navy lads.

The Broadway Follies entertainment group who kept Tolworth's spirits high during the war.

Norman and Edith Lewis with their son Peter, shortly before their move to Tolworth.

At the time of these concerts, singer Petula Clark was about nine years old and living in the area. She was managed by her father. She was invited to appear with the Broadway Follies to be billed as The Broadway Follies with Petula Clark. Her father strongly objected, saying she would only appear if the title read Petula Clark with the Broadway Follies. As neither would give way, she did not appear.

Norman Lewis was in a reserved occupation during the war due to his grocery experience but was engaged in fire-watching along with Miss Black, manageress of F.W. Woolworth's; Eric

Ward, manager of the RACS Dairy; Stan Deal, manager of Sainsbury's; and Harry Biggs among others.

Norman had strong political views quite left of centre. He had been influenced by seeing the suffering of the poor during the 1930s and he campaigned actively to support Republican Spain against Franco's fascists and stood as the Tolworth communist candidate at the 1947 elections and was elected by quite a large majority to become the only communist to win an election in Surrey up to that time.

The family lived in a flat above the shop but the bedrooms were at a higher elevation. The closeness to the night skies worried Edith Lewis. She had a rather nervous disposition and was unhappy about sleeping on the upper floors. Arrangements were therefore made for Harry Colley, the manager of Macfisheries store next door, his wife, Agnes, and their family to use the staff air raid shelter of Boots the Chemist. The Lewis family then were able to sleep in the Colleys' home.

Norman and Edith Lewis in post-war years. He was Surrey's only Communist councillor and police warned him he was in danger of being killed.

Norman's son, Peter recalled: "I well remember seeing hundreds of German bombers going overhead to bomb Coventry. Somehow we did not take the same precautions over the V1s and V2s as we did earlier in the war. Possibly we had become rather blase by 1944.

"It was quite a common occurrence for many of the shop windows in The Broadway to be smashed due to bomb blast and, strangely, little if any looting of goods from these windows took place.

"In the early months of 1940, particularly after Dunkirk, the threat of an invasion was very real and I well remember a knock on our front door and when opened, there was PC Bill Crompton, whose wife worked as shop assistant in my father's shop. He asked me to come in and I was told to go to my bedroom.

"Bill Crompton informed my father that as a communist, his name was on a secret list held by the police and would in all probability, be handed to the Germans if they invaded. This would have meant my father's certain death.

"My mother naturally became very concerned and tearful. My father said he would take any decision necessary when the Nazis arrived. Fortunately they did not. Bill Crompton was a good man and did what I thought was quite a risky kindness which was much appreciated.

"Opposite my father's shop was Blue Star Garages, although, to me, Blue Star were the 'new boys'. Prior to their arrival, the garage was run by a nice man, Fred Bullen, and was called Harley Motors. Fred was a canny businessman who, during late 1939 and 1940, totally filled his garage with just about every good car he could buy. For once petrol rationing was introduced, nobody wanted their cars and they were sold off quite cheaply to Fred, who not only filled the ground floor but literally stacked them one on top of the other and when the war was over and new cars were almost non-existent, he made a real killing, selling about 70 cars in three weeks. Some were sold for five or six times what he had paid for them in 1940. He was unable to insure them, however, so if a stray bomb had hit his garage, he would have lost the lot."

Tolworth Rise wreckage

Two bombs dropped on houses alongside the Kingston bypass in Tolworth on 9th September 1940. One severely damaged Nos 170-174 Tolworth Rise (above). The other, at No 138, badly damaged a garage. No-one was killed in either incident.

The extensive damage to 174 & 176 Tolworth seen from the back gardens.

German crew killed

Shot down

Unearthed: Tail fin with a Swastica.

A GERMAN Messerschmitt 15/LG1 (3298) was shot down by fighters during a sortie over Surrey on 9th September 1940. It crashed in flames on Maori sports ground, near Tolworth Court Farm, Worcester Park Road. Initially, ARP took it to be a Dornier 219.

Surbiton Mortuary records three dead, one being D.R.K. Gelferin, aged 23, of No 30, Wielandstrasse, Frankfurt al Main. Other two aged 19 and 20. The Battle of Britain Then and Now Book states only Uffz. Pfafflhuber and Uffz. Kramp killed. Messerschmitts usually only two-seaters. London Air Museum later dug out a tail fin bearing Swastika emblem.

Later excavation.

On 9th September 1940, a high-explosive bomb detonated in the front garden of Nos 118 & 120 Beresford Avenue, Tolworth. The blast blew out windows and wrecked the roofs of both these 1930s semis. On the other side of the road, a high-explosive bomb fell on the back of No 125, requiring Nos 123 & 125 to be demolished.

ARP posts

SURBITON borough was divided into 40 Air Raid Precautions (ARP) districts. They were:

- St Andrew's Square
- Portsmouth Road by Ravens Ait
- Claremont Road near clock tower
- Surbiton Hill Road/Avenue Elmers junction
- Eversley Road/Hill Crescent junction
- Upper Brighton Road, just south of the railway
- Langley Avenue/Ashcombe Avenue junction
- Ditton Road, western part
- Oakhill Crescent
- Ewell Road next to fire station
- Surbiton Hill Park
- Manor Drive
- The Byeways/Chiltern Drive junction
- Stirling Walk
- Present site of Edith Gardens
- Ditton Road/Ellerton Road junction
- Dennan Road
- Red Lion Road/School Lane junction
- Thornhill Road/Fullers Avenue junction
- Hook Road opposite Tolworth Road junction
- Fullers Avenue/Red Lion Road junction
- Oakcroft Road/Hook Rise South junction
- Hamilton Avenue/Ladwood Road junction
- Largewood Avenue near junction with Cranborne Avenue
- Tolworth Broadway opposite Catholic Church
- Beresford Avenue/Lyndhurst Avenue junction
- Elgar Avenue near junction with Elmbridge Avenue
- Barnsbury Crescent
- Oakdene Drive/Raleigh Drive junction
- Hunters Road/Priory Road, Hook
- Clayton Road near Cricketers, public house, Hook
- Mansfield Road, west of Hartfield Road
- Rhodrons Avenue near Elm Road, Hook
- Between Grange Road and Orchard Road, Hook
- Bridge Road, western end
- Bolton Road near Ellingham Road
- Recreation Ground, Leatherhead Road, south of Garrison Lane
- Moor Lane/Bridge Road junction
- Gilders Road/Filby Road junction Ashby Avenue/Maltby Road junction
- Leatherhead Road, south of West Road.

Numbers 4 & 6 Oakleigh Avenue, Tolworth, (above) were both rendered uninhabitable and were pulled down after being smashed to pieces by the blast of a high-explosive bomb on 28th September 1940. Two other high-explosive shells wrought havoc in the street the same day. One went off at the rear of No 19, the other by No 23, severely damaging a garage and the rear of nearby shops. In the small hours of the next morning, tragedy struck in Largewood Avenue, Tolworth, when 45-year-old Jennie Cherg was killed by falling masonry as Nos 107, 109 & 111 were demolished by a powerful bomb. Next door, at No 111, the body of 50-year-old Gertrude Bingott was found. She had also been killed by collapsing masonry. Her body, like that of her neighbour, was found at 4.30am.

My schooldays

DAVID Wood (right) was a schoolboy in Lyndhurst Avenue, Egmont estate, Tolworth, during the war years, attending Tiffin Boys' School, Kingston, where he used to carry out weekend fire watch duties.

"During air raids we used to share the shelters in the school grounds with some of the female factory workers from nearby. They used to teach us card games."

The school had an anti-aircaft gun and on one occasion, at eight o'clock in the morning, it shot down an enemy plane.

Mr Wood recalled the simple life at home in those times. In winter, rooms were individually heated with coal fires, but this was normally restricted to the kitchen and another room. "Your warmth depended simply on how close you sat to the fire," he said. "It was a novelty, when ill, to see mum come into the bedroom with a bucket of coal and make a fire."

He recalled the icy weather of January 1940: "Waking up in the morning, you could sometimes see the windows covered in frost which you could scrape off with your finger nails and watch the snow-like stuff form at the bottom, on the sill. I remember the fun I had slowly blowing on the window to form a break in the frost to look out on to the garden through a little peep hole."

In the pages of his 1943 diary, he recalls the night-time air raids.

"The new Z-guns came to defend us and they used to light up the sky. During the day we used to see the huge fleets of American bombers and fighters going towards Germany and in the evening, the vast armada of British planes following them. One memorable evening, the two fleets crossed — the Americans coming home and the RAF going out. I don't think one will ever see so many aircraft in the sky at one time again."

During the Blitz in London, Tolworth also suffered bombardment. This was the scene at Nos 24, 26 and 28 Princes Avenue after a high-explosive bomb detonated in the road on 15th September 1940, rocking these 1930s homes and damaging water mains. The same day, another HE bomb caused similar devastation next to No 34 Princes Avenue.

A bomb exploded on 28th September 1940 at No 124 Douglas Road, by the junction of Ravenscar Road, Tolworth. The house was reduced to rubble and Elizabeth Kilne, aged 80, the occupant, was killed. The body was found at 12.45am that same night.

Victoria Avenue, Surbiton received three high-explosive blasts on 27th September 1940. In addition, an incendiary bomb dropped onto the roof of No 39, damaging the roof and burning the floor. The HE bombs fell on No 19, causing slight damage; on No 11a, which suffered on the same scale; and No 7 which was demolished. Nos 5 & 9 were extensively damaged. Pictured above are Nos 5, 7 and 9 Victoria Avenue.

Three killed in Vincent Avenue

Four homes on the Sunray estate, Tolworth, were flattened by a high-explosive bomb going off on 28th September 1940 during the tense early days of the Blitz in London. Nos 33, 35, 37 and 39 Vincent Avenue came crashing down in the wake of the blast. The bomb had landed on No 35 & 37 in the road, built in the early 1930s to provide affordable housing in the Surbiton borough. Three residents were killed. They were 70-year-old Elizabeth Annie Dunnage, of No 37, who was discovered at 11.45am the next morning; Dorothy Kathleen Dunnage, 25, of the same address, found at the same time; and Kathleen Mary Dwyer, 75, of No 39, whose body was located at 2.50pm that afternoon. The deaths were all attributed to falling masonry.

Blast damage from a high-explosive bomb falling in Pyne Road, Tolworth, on 28th September 1940, resulted in the demolition of Nos 23, 25 & 27 in the Victorian street off Red Lion Road. The bomb had landed on No 23. Further HE bombs descended the same day in Red Lion Road itself, demolishing Nos 95-99; and at Lenelby Road where the Royal Windsor laundry was considerably damaged. Three houses in Draycott Road were also hit in the raid and Nos 6 & 8 were flattened.

Damp, smelly shelter lit by paraffin lamp

I slept in a cupboard

BORN in 1937, Joyce Spires was just two years old when the Second World War was declared. She remembers being carried downstairs by her father, Cecil, and taken through the back garden to the shelter next door in Southcote Avenue, Tolworth. She had to go down a few steps to get into the shelter.

"It had a corrugated tin roof and was then covered with earth and grass grown on top, recalled Joyce in later life. "There were wooden bench seats around the side and back and it was lit by a paraffin lamp. It was very damp and smelly and eight of us used to squeeze into the shelter. Five from our family and three from the Wooton family."

Later, Mr Spires and his wife, Katie, had an indoor shelter constructed in their front room. They slept there with their two sons while Joyce spent the night in the cupboard under the stairs. A light was left on during the night and the door was kept shut.

Joyce Spires aged 12.

"I can remember watching the buzz-bombs coming over and when they cut out, seeing them go down and my father saying some poor soul has 'had it'," said Joyce, reflecting on the events of 1944 nearly six decades later at her home in Rhiwbina, Cardiff, which she has shared with her husband, Peter Lewis.

"We went to see the damage and destruction that was caused when some houses were hit close to Red Lion Road near the isolation hospital. I understand some of the inhabitants were killed."

Joyce may well have been recalling a visit to see the devastation in Tolworth Park Road, off Red Lion Road, on 17th June 1944 when 12 people lost their lives.

Nos 53 & 55 Alpine Avenue, Tolworth, after a devastating bomb fell on 29th September 1940.

"A bomb also dropped near Surbiton Lagoon and we had a few windows blown out of our house."

It was after this that the younger of Joyce's two brothers, her mother and herself were sent to stay with relatives in Cambridge until the worst of the bombing was over.

Mr Spires worked in the civil service in London and he used to have to carry out night watch duty. He would cycle 12 miles to work and back again each day in every sort of weather imaginable. If he had a puncture, he would bring his bike into the kitchen to repair it ready to leave for work early next morning.

Joyce clearly remembers the use of ration books.

"I used to go shopping with my mother most days and queue at the different counters in the Co-op and Sainsbury's on the Broadway for our few provisions. And every Saturday morning a friend and I would go with our weekly quota of coupons to the sweet shop on the corner of Elgar Avenue to get a two-ounce packet of Maltesers each.

"I also had a Mickey Mouse-style gas mask which I hated putting on. I can remember screaming the house down when trying it out when it first arrived.

"After the war, we had a street party in Northcote Avenue which involved Southcote Avenue, Endway, Ruston Avenue, and Sandhurst Avenue. We had races and throwing a tennis ball as far as you could, which I won for my age group."

Six homes in Alpine Avenue on Tolworth's new Sunray estate had to be demolished after suffering a direct hit from one of the enemy's high-explosive bombs on 29th September 1940. They were Nos 47-57 Alpine Avenue. Two people died from falling masonry.

Braemar Cottage, Surbiton Hill Road, was demolished by a high-explosive bomb on 2nd October 1940. The property was used as a store. Surbiton Hill Road links the Assembly Rooms and the Waggon and Horses public house with the top of St Mark's Hill.

The shell of St Mark's Church, Surbiton, after the fierce blaze on 2nd October 1940. Note the trolley bus wires.

Nazi bombs set church ablaze

St Mark's on fire

TWO high-explosive Nazi bombs and an oil bomb rained down on St Mark's Hill, Surbiton, on 2nd October 1940 at the height of Hitler's Blitz on London.

St Mark's Church, was burnt out and partly demolished.

In the early hours, a "terrific" explosion resulted from one of five bombs to fall in the neighbourhood. One bomb struck the middle of the church roof and as the massive wooden beams crashed, they became a mass of flames.

The vicar, Reverend John Halet, aroused by the shaking of his vicarage, hurried out to find his church in ruins and blazing furiously. The "spacious and dignified" interior was wrecked but the walls and spire withstood the attack. The clock remained chiefly intact, but its hour hand "had been given a twist".

The vicarage garden also received a hit. Remarkably, virtually no damage occurred.

A raid three days previously had caused splinters to damage the windows of St Andrew's Church, Surbiton.

St Mark's had been standing since 1845 and could seat 590 adults and 130 children before it was rebuilt with a new tower in the 1850s after which it could accommodate more than 1,000 worshippers. The parish of St Mark's had been created out of the former larger parish of All Saints, Kingston.

Air raid wardens on fire patrol arrived speedily at the scene of the burning church but were unable to prevent the flames from engulfing the building. A shortage of water in the mains also hampered the firefighters.

The church was later reconstructed.

An altar cross survives untouched in St Mark's Church, Surbiton, destroyed by bombing on 2nd October 1940.

The devastated western end of St Mark's Church, Surbiton, after the bombing raid of 2nd October 1940.

Surbiton resident Douglas Bond at the age of 74 in 2002 examines a cairn made of stone from St Mark's Church, Surbiton, bombed on 2nd October 1940. The cairn is in the garden of the war memorial, Ewell Road, Surbiton.

Not even the memorial to those who fell in the First World War was spared from the effects of the blast and blaze at St Mark's Church. Hundreds of Surbiton residents came to see the smouldering ruins of the church in the wake of the fire. Schoolboy Douglas Bond was among them.

Bombing near Avenue Elmers

The wreckage of No 31 St Mark's Hill, Surbiton, partially destroyed on 2nd October 1940 by a bomb – one of four to fall that day in the vicinity of St Mark's Hill. This was the view from Avenue Elmers. On the same day, too, three lives were lost at Chessington Zoo in the shelter trenches. Five high-explosive bombs detonated and one hit an air raid shelter, fatally injuring Mrs E Arnold, aged 55; Mrs Annie Page, 35, and 10-year-old Ronnie Page.

The Blitz in London continued unabated throughout October 1940. On October 12th, an unexploded bomb smashed through The Beacon, Nos 7 & 7a Surbiton Hill Park, rendering it beyond repair. A number of neighbouring properties were damaged.

The extent of damage caused by the UXB at The Beacon was considerable.

The scene of destruction in Eversley Road, Surbiton, following an air raid on 12th October 1940 which claimed three lives.

Three killed as homes reduced to rubble

Eversley Road fatalities

Three people lost their lives when a high-explosive bomb rocked the Eversley Road neighbourhood close to Villiers Avenue, Surbiton. Nos 9, 11, 13 & 15 Eversley Road were demolished by the explosion and houses over a wide area required extensive repairs following the blast on 12th October 1940.

Mrs Emily Alexander, aged 65, Miss Kathleen Alexander, 29, and Mr Thomas Ore, 70, all of No 13, were killed. Their bodies were discovered in the wreckage at 6pm the next day and conveyed to Surbiton Mortuary.

At the start of the war, Edgar Matthews lived at No 9; William Holt at No 7; Philip Alexander at No 13; and Alex Eagle at No 15 with other members of their families.

Other neighbours included Harold Goodrich at No 1; Reginald Baker at No 3; Andrew Griffiths at No 17; William Dale at No 19 and James Ward at No 21. William Rayner resided at No 23.

Eversley Road leads from Villiers Avenue to Burney Avenue. Roads off it include Hill Crescent, Minniedale, Guilford Avenue, Ferguson Avenue, Chumleigh Walk and Cheyne Hill.

The ruins of Nos 9, 11, 13 and 15 Eversley Road after the explosion on 12th October 1940. Hill Crescent can be seen ahead with the roof of one of the houses covered in tarpaulin.

An air raid shelter behind Nos 9-15 Eversley Road, Surbiton, showing the damaged houses in Ferguson Avenue, after the blast on 12th October 1940. Their skeletal roofs can be made out.

The same view from No 13 Eversley Road today.

Both Nos 5 & 7 Pyne Road, off Red Lion Road, Tolworth, were reduced to ruins after the blast from a high-explosive bomb severely rocked both homes on 15th October 1940. The road backs onto Lenelby Road which housed the Royal Windsor Laundry, seriously damaged inside by another bomb three weeks earlier on 28th September.

A high-explosive bomb exploded on open ground between Nos 81 & 85 Red Lion Road, Tolworth, on 15th October 1940, leaving properties nearby in a sorry state. This was No 87 Red Lion Road. Note the three horseshoes above the front door of the neighbour's house, which was lucky not to have been more badly affected.

The Auxiliary Fire Service members who were based at the Harley Motors Site at the junction of Tolworth Broadway and Ewell Road during the 1939-45 war. They used to whistle at attractive passing girls during lulls in their fire-fighting operations in Surbiton, Tolworth and Hook.

The Crossways parade of shops on the corner of Ewell Road, Warren Drive and Raeburn Avenue bore the brunt of the devastation from a high-explosive bomb which fell from the skies on 15th October 1940. Shop fronts caved in and scores of windows shattered.

The junction of Warren Drive and Beresford Avenue, Tolworth, showing Nos 21 & 23 Warren Drive after a high-explosive bomb blast on 15th October 1940. Serious damage to property was spared but utility service-pipes under the road were ruptured.

Three members of the Home Guard based at the Electric Light Works, Hollyfield Road, Surbiton.

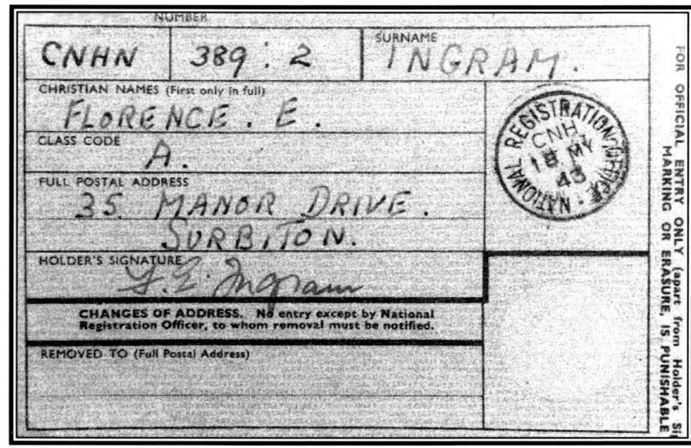

NUMBER
CNHN 389 : 2
SURNAME INGRAM.
CHRISTIAN NAMES (First only in full)
FLORENCE . E .
CLASS CODE
A.
FULL POSTAL ADDRESS
35. MANOR DRIVE.
SURBITON.
HOLDER'S SIGNATURE F. E. Ingram
CHANGES OF ADDRESS. No entry except by National Registration Officer, to whom removal must be notified.
REMOVED TO (Full Postal Address)
NATIONAL REGISTRATION OFFICE CNH 18 MY 43
FOR OFFICIAL ENTRY ONLY (apart from Holder's Si
MARKING OR ERASURE, IS PUNISHABLE

Florence Ingram's National Identity Card. Everyone required one in the war.

Grocery shops such as S. Frost & Co Ltd, Claremont Road, Surbiton, had to learn to deal with the system of rationing supplies during the war years. Families were handed ration books with coupons to make sure that all had a fair share of the dwindling foodstuffs, such as sugar and fats that were still available. This photo was taken just before the war. Third from the right is shop assistant Florence Edith Ingram, who lived for 55 years at 35 Manor Drive, Surbiton.

Homes in the vicinity of the Kingston bypass and the railway line through Tolworth, Berrylands and Surbiton appeared to be at greater risk from air raids. A high-explosive bomb demolished Nos 285, 287 289 & 291 Hook Rise, Tolworth, (above) on 17th October 1940. Hook Rise and Tolworth Rise formed part of the ribbon development next to the A3 after its construction in the late 1920s. Factories alongside, including Mollarts Engineering and Siebe Gorman, were targeted by the enemy planes.

Trapped in Anderson shelter at Hook Rise

People were trapped in an Anderson shelter when a second devastating high-explosive bomb in Hook Rise on 19th October 1940 rendered these homes at Nos 127, 129 & 131 uninhabitable. A rescue team worked hard to free those buried under the rubble. Miraculously no lives were lost.

Tolworth Isolation Hospital, Red Lion Road, was not spared. The operating theatre was hit on 17th November 1940.

Nine months before their untimely deaths, Ronnie and Annie Page are seen here at Woodview Cottages, No 23, Fairoak Lane, after the marriage of Ronnie's aunt, Joan Knight to Arthur Skilton, in the bitter, snowy January of 1940.

Mother and son killed in zoo shelter

CHESSINGTON Zoo keeper Reg Page was out on Home Guard patrol at Fairoak Lane when an enemy aircraft flew over his cottage in the zoo grounds, dropping a high-explosive bomb on 2nd October 1940.

As he was away from home, his wife, Annie, and son, Ronnie, chose to take refuge in the larger, L-shaped shelter with other zoo employees, rather than stay in a shelter closer to their home.

That decision proved fatal. For the main shelter took a direct hit from the bomb. In the aftermath of the blast, Mrs Page, 35; Ronnie, 10, and keeper's wife Mrs E Arnold, 55, of the Lodge in the zoo grounds, were found dead under the rubble.

Ronnie and Annie Page, who were killed in the shelter at the zoo.

Mrs Page was described by her cousin Mrs Chris Patey, as a very happy woman.

"She always had a laugh and was great fun."

She said her aunt and cousin had taken shelter in the main shelter, rather than their own Anderson shelter because they felt safer with other zoo staff. Both are buried at St Mary's Church.

Reg later joined the army, and after the war worked at the relocated zoo in Paignton, Devon, until it returned to Chessington. Some years later, he remarried.

Two high-explosive bombs shattered the peace of leafy Lovelace Road, Surbiton, on 26th October 1940. One fell into a garden near the rear of No 32 (above). The other went off 40 yards to the rear of the same house, rocking the mansion so violently it was well-nigh demolished. Neighbouring properties at Nos 28 & 30 were structurally damaged by the blast.

Guildown, No1 Ashcombe Avenue, Surbiton, near Woodlands Road, was wrecked by a high-explosive bomb detonating in the garden on 28th October 1940.

Severe damage occurred in Lovelace Road for a second time in a week when another high-explosive bomb shattered No 29. The bomb had gone off in the garden on 28th October 1940. Neighbours also suffered.

No 36 Lovelace Road after the air raid at No 29 on 28th October 1940.

Repair work was needed at No 31 Lovelace Road after 28th October 1940.

On 3rd November 1940, a bomb lay unexploded for eight hours after smashing into No 78 Ewell Road. It then went off dramatically.

Receptionist at Andre Rubber Company

Teenager's war years

HAVING lived at No 4 Sunray Avenue, Tolworth, from 1933 to 1945, Eileen Pepperell has poignant memories of the war years.

She left Tolworth Central Girls' School at the age 14, and started work in the general office of Harding's Pye Works at Acre Road, Kingston. She earned 12s 6d (63p) a week and was there when war was declared in September 1939.

"I do remember the first air raid warning. It was a Sunday morning, and my brother and I were on one of our walks down the Hogsmill, a regular past-time of our family. My mother (*Lilian*) was frantic until we returned, but, of course, it was a false alarm," recalled Eileen, then Eileen Malcolm.

She then progressed to receptionist and telephonist at the Andre Rubber Company alongside the Kingston bypass at Tolworth. By now her salary was 15s (75p) a week. The firm made tank tyres.

"I can still smell the rubber that always pervaded the factory floor," said Eileen in retirement at Shoreham-by-Sea.

During the early part of the war, the factory installed equipment to play music while its employees toiled away. There was a wireless and staff brought in their favourite 78rpm gramophone records.

In 1940, Eileen trained to work as a GPO telephonist and left for training in the City Telephone Exchange, London. During air raids, people were arriving with their belongings to spend the night in the underground stations. Eileen travelled to and from Tolworth and sometimes would have to stay in the Anderson shelter in the back garden at Sunray Avenue. It had been installed by a kindly neighbour, Jack Lee, of No 10 with the help of Eileen's father, who had an artificial leg as a result of the injuries he sustained in the Great War.

"My mother would prepare a flask and she had an empty Blue Bird toffee tin with all her personal documents in. It was kept by the back door ready to take with her when the siren sounded. We had bunk beds and often spent the whole night down there. I hated sleeping there. Occasionally I would sneak out to sleep in my own bed. Being young, I wasn't aware of the dangers.

"Rationing soon started to bite but mothers were incredible how they improvised. I can't ever remember being hungry. Meat was rationed but could be supplemented with rabbit, liver, hearts and sausages which were all unrationed, but often had to be queued up for. They did introduce whale meat but I did not like that at all.

"We did dig up our back lawn and grew potatoes, runner beans, and salads which were a great help. Of course, dried egg, dried milk, and spam was also available. Camp coffee was another useful addition and we made fat-less coffee cake. I can't remember how, but these things helped feed us.

Being in her teens, Eileen began to socialise. She enjoyed the cinema and ballroom dancing. She would go with her brother, Derek, to the Catholic Hall, opposite Tolworth Broadway, on Saturday nights. There was always a live band and a master of ceremonies to control the dancing. Waltzes, the foxtrot, and quick-step were popular and pairs were allowed to dance to three tunes each.

Derek joined the air force in 1941 and Eileen became a telephonist at the Emberbrook exchange in Thames Ditton. She missed dancing so attended the Carl and Jane Spencer School

George Pepperell married Eileen Malcolm, at St Matthew's, Surbiton, on 28th October 1944.

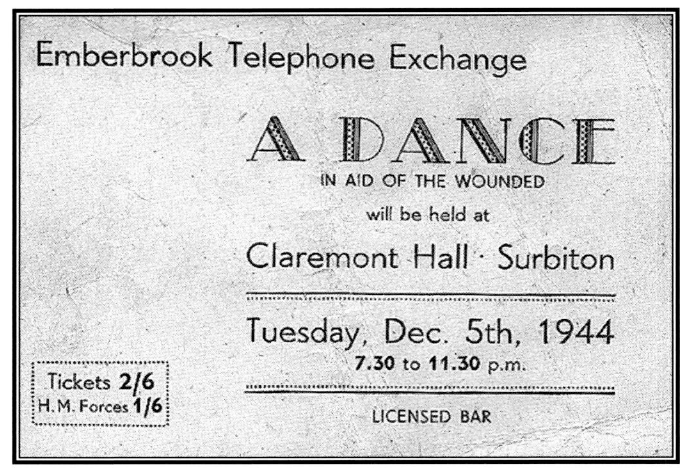

Emberbrook Telephone Exchange

A DANCE

IN AID OF THE WOUNDED

will be held at

Claremont Hall · Surbiton

Tuesday, Dec. 5th, 1944

7.30 to 11.30 p.m.

Tickets 2/6
H.M. Forces 1/6

LICENSED BAR

Charity events like this one in Claremont Hall, organised by Eileen Pepperell, helped the wounded.

George Pepperell and Eileen Malcolm on the island in Sunray Avenue, Tolworth, 1943.

The SPENCER-BRYANT
School of Dancing
80-81, Victoria Road, Surbiton

168

SUNDAY CLUB

MEMBERSI'IP CARD

Name M. G. Pepperell.

VALID UNTIL 31ST DEC., 1942

George Pepperell was a keen member of the Spencer-Bryant School of Dancing in Surbiton.

of Dancing in Victoria Road, Surbiton. It was here she met her husband-to-be, George Pepperrel. He, too, was a keen dancer.

In those days, boys and girls often met their future partners at dancing halls such as the ones in Surbiton.

Eileen also made lifelong friends with a girl called Nan. She provided good company when George joined the Air Force.

"It was quite common during the war years for two girls to dance together and Nan was very good at taking the lead. Her boyfriend, John, lived along the Brighton Road and his mother ran a cafe," recalled Eileen.

"The four of us became great friends as we would go to the football matches — Chelsea and Fulham — on a Saturday afternoon and go back to John's cafe for tea. It was there I first saw ham on the bone during the war. We would have that with chips. A great treat.

"When my boyfriend and I continued to take dancing medals, and when he was home on leave from the Air Force, we had some very happy times.

"The air raids did not seem to worry us. I suppose we were young and in love, but we were aware of the disasters in and around Tolworth.

"We did have an incendiary bomb at the back of the garden in Sunray Avenue, and my boyfriend and his family had to evacuate their home one night when bombs fell in Thornhill Avenue. They lived at No 110 and there were unexploded bombs at No 116 and in Bond Road around the corner.

"We eventually got engaged in 1943 and George was training to be an air gunner. I was still at Emberbrook Exchange and my mother started working at Fox and Nicholls, which by then was a small factory *(by the Kingston by-pass opposite Tolworth Odeon)*. My mother and her neighbour, Mrs Pat Boehm, of No 6 Sunray Avenue, worked on capstan machines doing war work.

"At the exchange, we worked a shift rota system and one of the shifts was 12.15 - 10.50pm and the next morning from 6.30am to 12.15pm. As we couldn't get home, we slept in the exchange on bunk beds. The night shift was always done by the male telephonists. Emberbrook and Surbiton's Elmbridge Exchange, were the old manual type of telephone systems. Calls were signalled by small lamps and the calls connected by the operators. It was always very busy during the war years and there were degrees of priority to be answered — military, war business, hospitals and police. Ordinary subscribers had to wait until last. After an air raid, the switchboards would be a blaze of lights — every one wanting to use their telephones.

"During the bombing it became very difficult. People would get irate and we had to take abuse from some."

Eileen and George got engaged at Christmas 1943 and arranged a wedding within three weeks, since George was posted to Canada for training as a rear gunner. The service was at St Matthew's Surbiton and Mrs Dorothy Cox of No 2 Sunray Avenue made the dress for the bride and the bridesmaids.

"With the rationing still on I can't imagine how we got the clothing coupons and the ingredients to make an iced cake for the wedding."

The Pepperells returned to St Matthew's Church on their 58th wedding anniversary.

Recalling the wartime blackouts

EILEEN Pepperell can well recall the blackouts during the war. Car headlamps were screened and dark curtains had to be pulled across lit rooms to confuse German pilots as to their location.

Eileen remembers:" We soon got used to the blackout and often walked home from Surbiton, Kingston and Ditton to Sunray Avenue, Tolworth, without problems. There seemed to be no vandalism or mugging those days. Traffic lights were covered first of all, leaving a little cross in the centre and head lights were partially covered."

She added: "Apart from growing vegetables in the back garden, we kept a few chickens and the eggs were very welcome and a Christmas dinner was always assured. Every house had a bucket and a stirrup pump in case of fire. Luckily we didn't need it."

Fifteen Victorian cottages in Richmond Grove, Surbiton, were condemned after a bomb shook them to their foundations on 3rd November 1940. The blast also damaged a hall nearby.

Frederick William White, aged 62, was killed when Nos 9, 10, 11 and 12 Guilford Villas, Surbiton, were demolished by a high-explosive bomb on 3rd November 1940. He was fatally wounded by falling masonry. Pictured are the remains of Nos 7 & 9 Guilford Villas.

A Christmas tragedy in Surbiton

Villiers Close fatalities

Christmas festivities in 1940 turned into a tragedy for residents in Villiers Close. In one air raid on 27th December, three people lost their lives in the cul-de-sac, off Lower Marsh Lane, at the foot of Villiers Avenue, Surbiton.

Four houses at Nos 15, 16, 17 & 18 were reduced to a pile of ruins by the high-explosive bomb dropping on Nos 16 & 17. In addition, Nos 11, 12, 12a, 14, 19 & 20 were considered uninhabitable and demolition was felt to be necessary.

The dead included David John Skelton, aged seven, of No 20. His body was found at 10pm that day. The other two casualties were Mrs Ethel Nash, aged 48, of No 18; and 30-year-old Mrs Ellen Bicknell, of No 16, who was not discovered until next day.

A fourth fatality occurred as a result of blast damage in Addison Gardens. Mrs Ellen Marsh, aged 71, of No 61, died four days later from the effects of the blast and shock.

Homes in Cheyne Hill were also badly damaged.

Staff at the United Dairies in Lower Marsh Lane used to take refuge in the shelters in a field at the back of the dairy. Close by were the 41 horses stabled for the milk delivery rounds in Surbiton. Apart from losing his wife of three years when a bomb wrecked his home at No 18 Villiers Close, the stablekeeper, Stanley Nash, lost an arm but somehow managed to carry on with his work after being hospitalised.

Sometimes the office staff at the dairy stayed in the shelters where they carried on working with adding machines.

At the time of the great Docklands blitz in London, one employee Joyce Eggleton, had a puncture in her bicycle wheel and could not get back to her home in Red Lion Road, Tolworth. She was allowed to stay in the dairy shelter. The Thames-side raid was at its height and by dawn, when it was safe for her to go home after her long Saturday shift, she saw the skies take on an orangy hue from the great fires of London.

Throughout that bombing campaign, the frightened horses were frantic and making a terrific noise.

Part of the wreckage of Nos 12a, 14, 15 & 16 Villiers Close, Surbiton — bombed on 27th December 1940.

Nos 17,18,19 & 20 Villiers Close, Surbiton, caught the full force of the blast from a high-explosive bomb on 27th December 1940. Inset: An Air Raid Precautions (ARP) cap badge worn by fire warden Ernest Howell, a father-of-two, of No 60 Villiers Avenue.

Nos 19 & 20 Villiers Close were wrecked by the blast from a high-explosive bomb. Inset: Modern day Villiers Close.

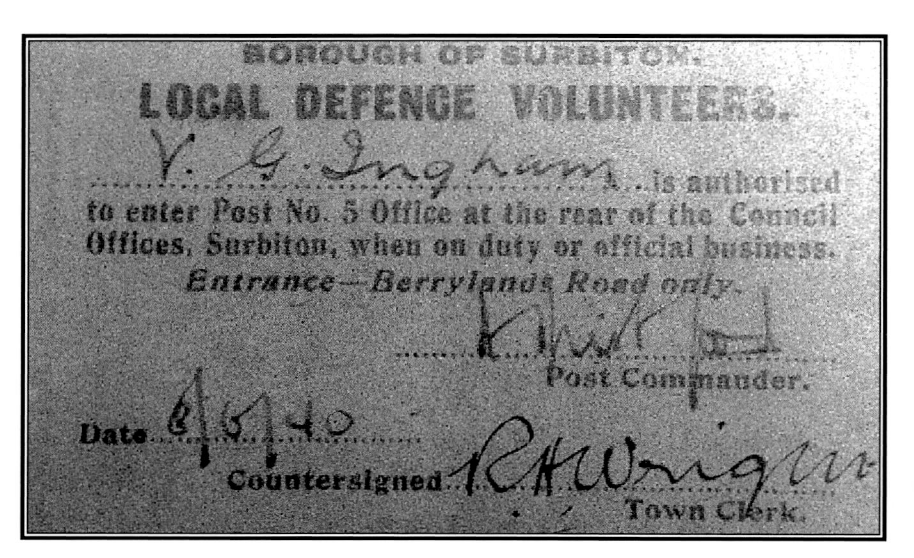
BOROUGH OF SURBITON.
LOCAL DEFENCE VOLUNTEERS.
V. G. Ingham ....is authorised
to enter Post No. 5 Office at the rear of the Council
Offices, Surbiton, when on duty or official business.
Entrance—Berrylands Road only.
....
Post Commander.
Date 8/6/40..........
Countersigned..........
Town Clerk.

Victor Ingram, of 35 Manor Drive, Surbiton, was one of many who joined the Local Defence Volunteers based at Berrylands Road. The LDV later became known as the Home Guard. This identity card was issued to Mr Ingram on 8th June 1944.

Air raid patrols and 'Dad's Army'

Victor and a colleague.

SURBITON was divided into 40 Air Raid Precautions districts, which would have ARP posts built of brick or concrete. There would be a protected area inside with a telephone, locker and lighting. If room permitted, there would be a store and rest room. Specially constructed posts would have a staff of three personnel.

Each district, or sector, would have a number of wardens — the civilian equivalent of a beat bobby in effect — under the supervision of the post warden. Most were unpaid volunteers, working part-time for about 48 hours each month, although many toiled for longer hours.

The full-time paid male wardens earned £3 per week; the females £2. The age of equality had not yet arrived.

Many rehearsals of the various services took place and Raeburn Avenue became the scene of an ARP training film in December 1939, complete with 'injured' people and the like.

Many factories deployed 'roof spotters' as well, who would raise an alarm during air raids.

All able-bodied men aged from 17-65 were called upon to join the Local Defence Volunteers on 14th May 1940. The LDV — to be named the Home Guard from July that year — would be the last line of defence, if invasion came, and indeed, battle seemed only weeks away.

Those men in the Home Guard were entitled to extra rations. After all, they were regarded as fighting men. Other personnel, such as messengers, incident officers, bomb reconnaissance officers (of which one in six were women) along with the fire services and Women's Voluntary Services, all played their part, with many roles overlapping.

The headquarters of Civil Defence in Surbiton was sited where the present British Red Cross Centre now stands in King Charles Crescent.

In September 1940, the Surrey Comet displayed an advertisement for reinforced concrete air raid shelters for £6, or £10 with delivery in three days. Anderson shelters made of corrugated iron, and half-submerged with earth in a back garden, gave some protection from bomb blast. When a bomb dropped on Hook Rise in October 1940, demolishing three homes, some residents were trapped in their shelter but their lives were spared.

Bravery was shown on many occasions. On 9th September 1940, for example, stretcher party leader L. Matthew was awarded the George Medal for rescuing a man trapped under a wrecked house.

A side view of the devastation at Nos 2 & 4 Chiltern Drive, Berrylands, after a high-explosive bomb blast on 11th January 1941.

The year before the Second World War broke out in 1939, residents of Douglas Road, Tolworth, who had their milk delivered by Job's Dairy in Tolworth, were rewarded with an outing to the the firm's bottling plant in Middlesex. Unknown to them when this photograph was taken, they were to suffer more than most in the area during the air raids. On one night alone in July 1941, a total of 14 bombs rained down on the road, killing six people and destroying several homes. Included in the picture are Mrs Page, Lillian Wells and her children — baby Alan and Doreen; Mrs May Heather, (fourth from left, front row) with her son, Eric, and daughter, Joan; Mrs Daisy Hiscock with Audrey and Gordon; Mrs Ellis, Jean and Valerie; Alfred Miller, Mrs Caseley and her daughter, Jean.

Wife and only child perish in ruins of bombed house

Disaster in Douglas Road, 1941

Victim: Ronnie Archer.

Victim: Violet Archer.

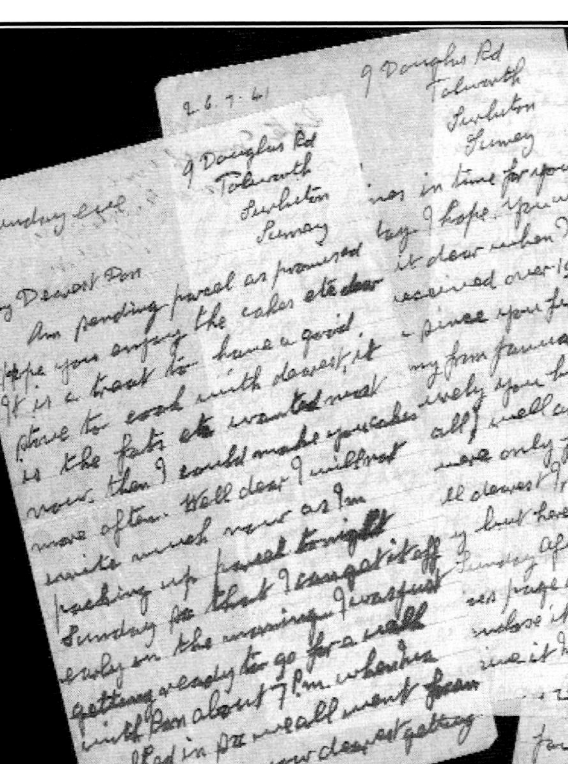

Letters Violet sent to her husband two days before she and Ron died.

Devoted wife Violet Archer counted the letters she had received from her beloved husband, Don, who had gone off to serve the country. In seven months he had sent 100 and she had kept them all.

On Sunday 26th July 1941, she wrote to her husband at the Catterick Barracks in Yorkshire and thanked him for being such a diligent letter-writer and not forgetting her and their only child Ronnie, aged nine.

Back home at No 9 Douglas Road, Tolworth, she had made him some cakes and that evening jotted down a note to go with the food parcel saying she hoped he would enjoy them.

That letter was to be her last. Two days later, their home took a direct hit from a German bomb.

Mrs Archer, 41, and her son were fatally wounded in the collapsing building.

Two neighbours living on the upper floor of the same rented house were also killed. They were sisters Jean and Barbara Strong, aged nine and five. Next door, at No 7, Annie Hurstwaite, 78, also died in the explosion which tore through Nos 5-13 Douglas Road.

In the penultimate letter, penned on the Sunday afternoon, Violet wrote: "My dearest Don. A few more lines in time for you to get on Monday, I hope. You will hardly believe it, dear, when I tell you I've received over 100 letters from you since you first started in the army from January. (You will say surely: 'You have not kept them all?').

"Have been busy cooking this morning but we both had breakfast, so I did not get a very early start. I have made some cakes for you, dear, and I will send on parcel tomorrow, or Tuesday.

"I packed our tea up to take out yesterday, but it was too wet. We went in and out of shops for a time then we decided to go to the Odeon in Kingston. We got in after waiting three-quarters of an hour in the queue. We got home at 8.20.

"Ma came in for the evening on Tuesday. One evening, she sat in here for two hours alone thinking I was out but I was busy down

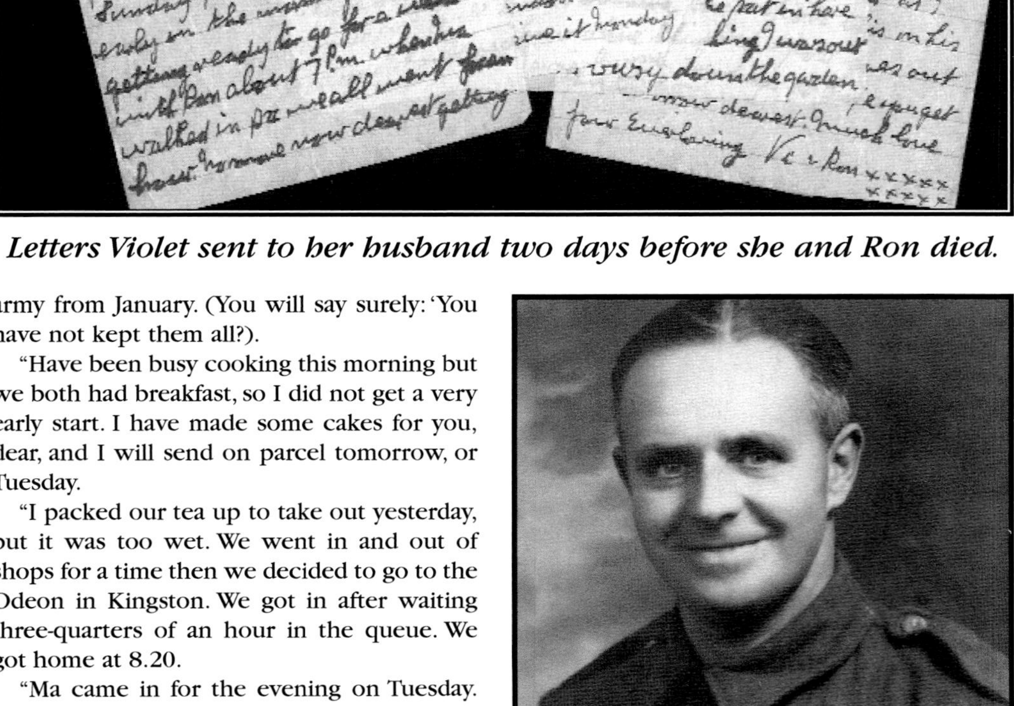

Widower: Don Archer.

Rescue workers examine the wreckage of Nos 5-13 Douglas Road, Tolworth, after the bomb on 28th July 1941 which killed five.

Douglas Road disaster - continued from page 50

the garden. I was on the look-out for her but I did not see her come, dear, and as I had left the back door open, I was surprised she did not think to come down the garden, as twice she had done that before.

"We have had a nice lot of rain but is bright and fine this afternoon, dearest, so I hope you will be able to get out today.

"Now I will close, dear, as I want Ron to post this on his way to church and the post goes out at 3.30 on Sundays, so hope you get this tomorrow, dearest. Much love, Your everlasting Vi and Ron XXXXX XXXXX."

Violet's final letter was written the same evening, after she had packaged up the cakes to send to Don.

"My dearest Don, am sending parcel as promised. Hope you enjoy the cakes etc, dear. It is a treat to have a good stove to cook with, dearest. It is the fats etc wanted most now, then I could make you cakes more often.

"Well, dear, I will not write much now as I'm packing up parcel tonight, Sunday, so that I can get it off early in the morning. I was just getting ready to go for a walk with Ron about 7pm when Ma walked in, so we all went for an hour.

"No more now, dearest, getting late. Much love, Your Everloving Vi and Ron XXXXXXXXXX."

Don, a butcher before he went into service, never really got over his wife and child's untimely deaths. He had told surviving relatives that Ron was a little seven-year-old with a mischievous streak. Don went on to perform war service in Belgium, Holland and elsewhere. In 1947, Don met a woman called Nancy in Bournemouth, married, and inherited step-daughters and a step-son, Trevor, who went on to become joint minister of Chessington Evangelical Church. In 2002, Trevor and his wife, Val, were still in residence at 46, Elmcroft Drive, Hook.

After the war, Don returned to Tolworth to live for many years at 44 Fullers Avenue. He worked on the buses out of Norbiton and Leatherhead garages — often on route 65. He died in March 1994 at the age of 87 and is buried next to his first wife, Violet. Nancy died in 1970. There were no children from the second marriage so Ron had remained his only child.

Nos 7, 5 & 3 Douglas Road rebuilt.

The ruins of Nos 5,7,9 & 11 Douglas Road after the air raid of 28th July 1941.

'My two daughters were killed, lest we forget . . .'

EVA Strong lost two daughters in the devastating bomb blast which brought down a row of houses in Douglas Road, Tolworth, on 28th July 1941.

Mrs Strong's rented flat on the first floor of No 9 suffered a direct hit from a German bomb. Her daughter, Jean, aged nine, and Barbara, five, perished as the house crumbled into a pile of ruins.

Mrs Strong, her husband and young son, aged three, were all injured in the explosion, which also claimed the life of Mrs Violet Archer, on the ground floor, and her son, Ron, nine, and neighbour Annie Hurstwaite at No 7.

For five months, Mrs Strong was kept in hospital with serious injuries. Her husband survived and lived to the age of 82.

Mrs Strong, in retirement at Fleetwood Close, Chessington, in the 1980s, felt aggrieved that so little was made of the Surbiton and Tolworth civilians whose lives were lost during the Second World War.

In a letter to the Surrey Comet, she wrote: "My husband paid tax on his pension to the day he died, taking nothing from the country except five war medals from two wars he need not have gone to because of his age.

"He joined the army at the age of 15, signing on for four years. At 16, he was a gunner and driver in the Royal Horse Artillery in France.

"When war ended, he had one year to serve and he volunteered to go to North Russia and fought against the Communists. When his year was up, he returned home and later joined the Royal Irish Constabulary. When this was disbanded, he came home to England at the start of the last war and joined the Home Guard and worked in an aircraft factory.

"When he recovered from his injuries received in the air raid at Douglas Road, he was called up, and after a short training course in North Africa, joined the fighting again, and was away for four years.

"That arrogant young man in the news, holding up Hitler's hat for sale, would hardly forget the war, as he said, if he had suffered as we did — and I still do for my children. He would not have been born but for the men who died, Hitler's belongings ought to have been destroyed as he destroyed so many lives."

Fourteen high-explosive bombs rained down on Douglas Road on 28th July 1941, in one of the worst local air raid attacks during the Second World War. Pictured is all that was left of Nos 30 & 32.

Toy shop family member killed

The rear of 306 Ewell Road, Tolworth, (left) after a high-explosive blast from one of 14 bombs to drop in the Douglas Road area on 28th July 1941 rocked the neighbourhood. Nature writer Richard Jefferies had lived at No 296 Ewell Road in the 1880s. His books included Nature Near London. Then, the row of mid Victorian villas was known as Woodside. Edith Trickey from the family toy shop, No 304 Ewell Road, was buried under falling masonry and was found dead at 2.40am. She was 51 years of age.

Pictured right is a side view of No 308 Ewell Road after the bombing raid of 28th July 1941. The location is next to the corner of Douglas Road. A modern view is pictured above after rebuilding.

The rear of Nos 298 & 300 Ewell Road, Tolworth, after the air raid of 28th July 1941. Edith Trickey, 51, whose family ran a toy shop here at the junction with Douglas Road, lost her life. She lived next door at No 304.

Separated from parents; mother ill, baby dies

Family plagued with grief

WHEN the Heather family were bombed out of their home in Douglas Road, Tolworth, it was just another cruel blow in a long sequence of unhappy events which had plagued their lives.

May Heather had suffered a dark and disturbing childhood in London and had been fostered out to people who did not want her. One of her foster mothers even committed suicide.

But there was eventually a ray of light after those difficult years. By chance, she met Dennis Heather on a bus and fell in love. Dennis, too, had been through troubled times.

He had lost both parents as a child — his father when he was six and his mother when he was 10. He was devastated for he had no brothers or sisters with whom to share the grief. His father had died from pneumonia in 1917 and his mother from an infection of the bone behind the ear which, in those days, often led to fatal brain damage.

After he was orphaned, Dennis had gone to live with a foster mother, but she, too, took her own life while he was in her care.

Dennis, a carpenter, and May, a cook in domestic service, married in December 1933 at West End, Chobham. He was 23 and she was 21.

Before the start of war, Dennis moved to Surbiton when he took employment with the Southern Railway, working as a carpenter and joiner.

He rented the upper floor of 54 Douglas Road, Tolworth, from a Mr Adams of Elgar Avenue. It was a terraced house like many of the other Victorian cottages in Douglas Road.

It had a dark stairwell, coloured glass in the front door and a seldom-used bathroom which contained a malfunctioning gas geyser. A galvanised bath hung in the kitchen.

On one occasion, May cooked her husband's supper, put it in the oven and when she went to fetch it noticed a mouse nibbling away at it. She went back to the oven, clutching her cat, but the pet refused to respond quickly enough and the mouse escaped at high speed.

On the ground floor lived Sam and Lois Bocking. He was a railwayman, but died during the Heathers' tenancy.

In August 1934, May gave birth to a baby son, Eric.

A year later, in July 1935, a daughter, Hilda, was born but

Dennis and May Heather outside No 54 Douglas Road on 11th May 1941 with their three children Eric, Edna and Joan. Ten weeks later, their home had been destroyed and soon after, sickly baby Edna died "from dust on the lungs".

tragedy was again to strike. The baby died in Tolworth at the age of three months and was buried at the church in West End, Chobham, where her parents had married less than two years earlier. The couple tried again for another baby and Joan was born on 2nd March 1937. Another daughter, Edna, was born on 16th March 1941 but, the pleasure of the new baby was to be short-lived. On 21st September she also died.

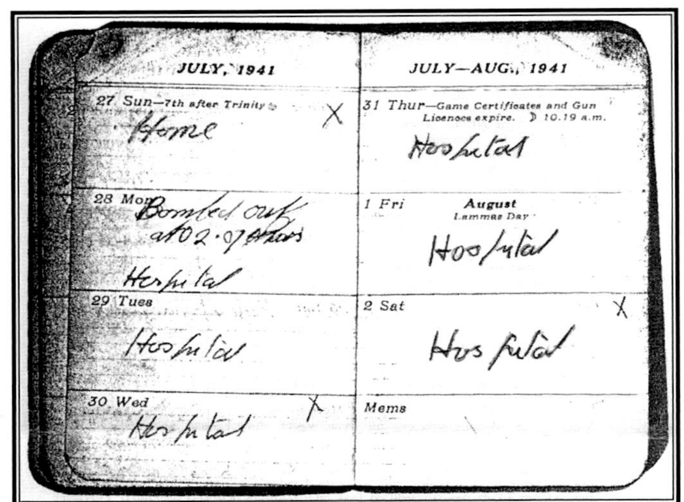

JULY, 1941

27 Sun—7th after Trinity
Home

28 Mon
Bombed out at 02.07 hours
Hospital

29 Tues
Hospital

30 Wed
Hospital

JULY—AUG., 1941

31 Thur—Game Certificates and Gun Licences expire. ☽ 10.19 a.m.
Hospital

1 Fri — August — Lammas Day
Hospital

2 Sat
Hospital

Mems

Dennis Heather's diary entries for the last week of July 1941, recording the bombing of his house and his resulting hospitalisation.

All this was on top of a new catalogue of catastrophes.

May's health was poor and she was later to suffer mental problems. Dennis was allowed to carry on working for the railways and was exempt from military service. He had also been told his wife could not be left alone. His work took him all over London, repairing war-damaged railway sites.

He also performed Air Raid Precautions duties in Tolworth and joined the St John Ambulance Brigade.

Increasingly, May became confined to hospital, and he was left to care for the children in addition to all his other duties.

In January 1941, the Heather siblings were despatched to Addlestone to be looked after but by April, their mother was back home at Douglas Road and on 7th June Eric was given a new face-piece for his gas mask. The family enjoyed several trips to the cinema — either the Coronation, Odeon or Empire.

Then disaster struck. At 2.07am on Monday 28th July 1941, a cluster of high-explosive bombs dropped on Douglas Road, killing six and flattening the Heather's home and others along the road. The family had been sleeping in the house and not in an Anderson shelter. Although the children were virtually unscathed, Dennis was hospitalised for three weeks and his wife for longer, suffering a broken pelvis and other crush injuries. Joan was taken to Surrey County Children's Home, 12 St Matthew's Avenue, Surbiton. Eric went to a similar concern

No 48 Douglas Road, Tolworth, collapsed in the 2am blast on 28th July 1941 which destroyed the Heather family's home at No 54. The site of No 48 was cleared and is now the driveway and garage of No 46 (left). Through the gap can be seen the tower of the primary school. Pictured (inset) is Lois Bocking, of No 54, who escaped the blast as she was performing ARP duties nearby.

at Palace Road, East Molesey.

Eric later recalled; "We both remember that as a miserable time and whatever may have been said to us, I don't think we understood what had happened to Mum and Dad.

"He twice called to see me at Molesey, but I was out on both occasions and didn't meet him until 27th September."

That was the day he was shown a new house the family would live in. No 189 Hamilton Avenue had been requisitioned by Surbiton Borough Council.

Three weeks earlier, baby Edna had died in Redhill Hospital. Her mother wasn't present at her death — being hospitalised at or near Surbiton. Edna was buried at Surbiton Cemetery but her mother was not well enough to be present at the funeral. The baby had suffered "dust on the lungs" after the blast.

The family stayed at Hamilton Avenue until 1949. The family had no money for furniture, but the Women's Voluntary Service provided much-needed items.

On 6th October, May had an operation, adding further to the huge family worries, but life assumed some normality four months after the bombing.

Dennis Heather's diary note for 21st November 1941 reads: "Brought May home. Obtained Ration Book, sent in milk-form, obtained discharge certificate."

On 29th November, after a renewed spell in Surbiton Hospital, May was taken to Douglas Road to see the remains of her old home.

Gradually, family life returned to normal. On Saturday 6th December 1941 after Eric was given a new identity card, the Heathers all went to Kingston and Eric and Joan attended a party. But he had to reserve some strength to carry out his air raid patrol the same evening.

In the subsequent years after the bombing, it was realised that May had suffered a psychological condition caused by the blast. She had virtually lost her voice for several years and uttered words only in a husky whisper. Her recovery, after the war, seemed miraculous.

In about 1943-4 Dennis was secretly drafted with 20,000 others to help build a huge harbour at Normandy.

The Heathers' widowed neighbour, 'Auntie' Bocking stayed with the family in Hamilton Avenue. Her home in Douglas Road was no longer standing after the bombing so the Heathers provided her with lodgings.

Dennis Heather became active politically. He subscribed to the Daily Worker, Daily Mirror, and Reynolds News and supported the Communist Party's candidate, Mr Clark, in Tolworth, attending the Daily Worker bazaar in the Co-op Hall, Tolworth Broadway.

Eric later wrote: "I was 10 years old, coming up 11, and had never quite realised that we were 'Labour'. I took to it with gusto and remember being rebuked, along with some other boys from Tolworth Juniors, by an indignant old lady outside Tilbury's, the baker's, on Tolworth Broadway, for shouting rude things about Mr Churchill. I shouted back that he was a "war monger", though I'm not sure I knew what it was. Dad had told us Churchill was a war monger and he had no time for the working man."

In later life, Dennis became an ardent member of Chessington Evangelical Church and became far more outgoing. He died in 1989 a year after his wife, May.

Eric went into the clergy and was ordained. He took on the position as honorary curate of St Paul's Church, Hook Road, Hook, and has been a popular personality in Hook.

As a child during the war, Doreen Wells, of Douglas Road, Tolworth, was spellbound every time she passed Trickey's toy shop near the corner of Ewell Road and Douglas Road. Christmas-time was even more of a draw. But the shop was bombed on 28th July 1941 and owner Edith Trickey, a small, plump lady, was killed. In later years, Doreen portrayed herself in this picture.

Memories

CHILDREN in Tolworth were magnetised to Trickey's toy shop. It stood at the corner of Douglas Road and Ewell Road.

Doreen Wells — now Conroy — recalls as a six-year-old stopping to look at the wonderful range of toys in the window as she passed, hand in hand, with her mother, on the way to St Matthew's School in Ewell Road.

The Trickey family also kept a dairy in Worthington Road.

Bert Trickey ran the shop but was not related to the Trickey toy distribution firm next to Ewell West Station.

Edith Trickey died when a high-explosive bomb fell on the shop and the flat above — at No 304 Ewell Road — on 28th July 1941.

The bomb was one of a batch of 14 that came down in the Douglas Road area in the small hours.

"It was a lovely little toyshop," said Doreen in retirement at Maythorn Cottage, in Thornhill Road, Tolworth.

Doreen's mother, Lilian, first moved to Tolworth in 1914.

The night of 700 fire bombs

Under attack: Bond Road, Tolworth, after the raid on 23-24th February 1944.

Bond Road, Tolworth, had its fair share of disruption when, on the night of 23rd February 1944, incendiary devices rained down on Surbiton, Tolworth and Berrylands, causing numerous fires which stretched the resources of Air Raid Precautions and the auxiliary fire service.

A 50-kilogram phosphorus incendiary device caused a slight fire in a garage at No 70, Bond Road, but the flames were put out by a trailer pump. There were no casualties.

A high-explosive 50kg bomb dropped at No 74, but apparently did not go off. It caused damage to mains in the road and a number of properites required repairs.

A further high-explosive bomb, which also failed to detonate, was discovered buried in the front garden of No 81. There were no casualties or damage.

Furthermore, another UXB was found in neighbouring Thornhill Road, at No 116, in the back garden. It was reportedly 250kgs, but later confirmed by the bomb disposal squad to be 50kgs. There was, again, no damage and no-one hurt.

Nearly 40 out of 669 incendiary bombs to fall in the borough ignited their targets, causing damage in Rose Walk, Surbiton Hill Park, Chiltern Drive, The Roystons, Berrylands, The Byeways, The Crest, The Ridings, The Ridge, Berrylands Road, King Charles Road, Manor Crescent, The Avenue, Surbiton Hill Park, Seymour Gardens, Chiltern Drive, Regent Road, and Berrylands Railway Station.

Many of the bombs fell through roofs, igniting loft spaces and upper bedrooms. At No 49 Berrylands Road, one entered through a fanlight, and plunged downstairs into a hall.

Surbiton bombing diary

(excluding Tolworth, Berrylands, Hook and Chessington)

CODE: HE = high explosive; OB = oil bomb; AA = anti-aircraft; UXB = unexploded bomb.

12th September 1940: Anti-aircraft damage, driveway, 92 Ditton Road.
15th September 1940: Garden of 156 King Charles Road — slight damage to property.
23rd September 1940: Two HE bombs, Sewage Works — no damage. Two AA, 9 Cranes Park — house partly damaged.
25th September 1940: Back of 98 & 100 Ellerton Road — no damage. Originally thought to be a HE; subsequently found by bomb disposal squad in 1941 to be a 1,000kg UXB.
27th September 1940: Incendiary bomb (IB) 39 Victoria Avenue — roof damaged and floor burnt. HE, 19 Victoria Avenue — slight damage. HE,11a Victoria Avenue — slight damage. HE, 7 Victoria Avenue — demolished. Junction of Portsmouth Road and Cadogan Road — damage to mains. HE, Portsmouth Road, opposite Grove Road — embankment wall demolished. 3 HE, Ravens Ait Island — no damage. IB, 41 Lovelace Gardens. Damage to roof. IB, 26a Lovelace Gardens — damage to roof. 20 Lovelace Road — slight damage. IB 23 Lovelace Road — damage to front of house. 2 HE, Surbiton railway embankment near Lovelace Road — damage to rail lines. HE, 17 Lovelace Gardens — demolition expected. Back garden of 20 Lovelace Gardens — damage to property.
29th September 1940: HE, Maple Road corner of St Andrew's Road — fractured water main. UXB, Rear of 2 Oakhill Road. Slight damage to stables. UXB, 4 Oakhill Road — removed by bomb disposal unit. UXB, 6 Grove Footpath — house demolished. HE, footpath by 23 Upper Brighton Road — slight damage only. UXB, Garden of Esher House, 8 Oakhill — no damage.
2nd October 1940: 2 HE, Railway embankment, Surbiton — no damage. HE Sewage Works — no damage. HE Store building of Braemar — demolished. 31 St Mark's Hill — demolished. HE & OB, St Mark's Church — burnt out. HE, grounds of St Mark's vicarage — no damage. HE, garden of 6 Adelaide Road. No damage. UXB and HE, grounds of Metropolitan Water Board — no damage/water main burst.
9th October 1940: HE, Filter bed, Fleece Road/Balaclava Road — extensive damage to windows in neighbourhood.
10th October 1940: HE, Victoria recreation ground, Balaclava Road — damage to water main, shelters flooded. HE, on railway by Victoria recreation ground. Train partly derailed. No casualties. HE, Victoria recreation ground, Long Ditton side.
11th October 1940: IB, 60 & 62 The Avenue, slight damage to property. IB, 48 Guilford Avenue — roof and bedroom burnt out. IB, 32 Eversley Road — roof and ceiling burnt. IB, Christ Church School, Britannia Road — air raid warden Woodhall injured on way to duty.
12th October 1940: HE, 9-15 Eversley Road — these properties demolished and houses over a wide area damaged.
14th October 1940: HE, north-east corner of Surbiton Cemetery — no damage.
22nd October 1940: HE, grounds of Shrewsbury House School. Damage to conservatory. HE, garden at rear of 106 Ditton Road — slight damage to property. OB, front of 102 Ditton Road — no damage. Shrewsbury House paddock — no damage.
26th October 1940: HE, in garden near rear of 32 Lovelace Road. HE, In garden 40 yards to the rear of 32 Lovelace Road — house to be demolished and 28 & 30 badly damaged.
3rd November 1940: HE, 9,10,11 & 12 Guilford Villas — all to be demolished. HE, back garden of 97 Ewell Road. Fifteen houses to be demolished in Richmond Grove. UXB, 78 Ewell Road — exploded eight hours later and 76 & 78 Ewell Road demolished.
6th November 1940: IB, railway embankment north, Upper Brighton Road. Hoarding burnt.
27th December 1940: HE, 16 &,17 Villiers Close. Nos 15,16,17,18, Villiers Close demolished. Nos 11,12,12a,14,19 & 20 Villiers Close to be demolished and considerable damage done to property in Villiers Close, Addison Gardens, and Cheyne Hill.
10th May 1941. HE, Open grounds of Fishponds, opposite J.E.A., Hollyfield Road Road — damage to windows only. HE, In fishpond in open grounds — no damage.
18th January 1943: UX AA, 4 Arlington Road — minor damage, partly exploded. UX AA 21 Walpole Road — exploded on first floor of property — considerable interior damage and extensive damage to tiles. UX AA, Vickers Armstrong, Glenbuck Road — damage to machinery. UX AA Lovelace Gardens — exploded in roadway outside. Blast effect on walls and windows. Ditton Road — exploded in roadway outside 41 — exposing gas and electricity service pipes and cable.
3rd March 1943: UX AA, plot 83, allotments, Burney Avenue. AA Shell, garden rear of 1 Britannia Road, believed to have exploded.
5th January 1944: AA shell, Surbiton Station in track. Reported to bomb disposal as unexploded. Confirmed exploded.
6th February 1944: 69 Villiers Avenue, 8 Eversley Road and 6 Surbiton Hill Park — damage by shell splinters.
23rd/24th February 1944: Nearly 700 incendiary devices showered over the Surbiton borough. Berrylands and Tolworth take the brunt of the damage. In addition, soda container fire bombs in the back garden of 11 Seymour Gardens and 16 The Ridge. About seven UXBs buried at Alexandra recreation ground allotments and one on cricket field. Four of them 500kg. Parachute flares found at 9 Villiers Close and in field east of Addison Gardens.
4th July 1944: V1, (doodlebug) Sewage Farm, Lower Marsh Lane — no casualties. Minor blast damage to filter bed.
21st August 1944: V1, (doodlebug) Balaclava Road — blast damage and casualties.
15th November 1944: V1, (doodlebug) Ashcombe Avenue. Warden Summers killed, house demolished. Widespread blast damage.

Tolworth, Berrylands and Kingston bypass raids — where and when the bombs fell

OUT of the 60 people who died in the borough of Surbiton during the 1939-45 war as a result of enemy action, 37 of them were from Tolworth. The neighbourhood suffered badly. One raid at Tolworth Park Road left 12 dead. The story is told elsewhere in this book. Another attack was at Douglas Road which claimed the lives of six people.

On **9th September 1940**, Tolworth was badly hit by a bombing campaign. The Air Raid Precautions observed that a high-explosive (HE) bomb was dropped on the corner of Ewell Road and the Kingston bypass and damaged the Surrey County Council material dump. The same day, an incendiary bomb exploded at No 9 Fairmead, causing slight damage to a bedroom. An HE device exploded in the road outside No 12 Highfield Avenue, resulting in slight blast damage to nearby homes.

At Hook Rise, A high explosive bomb ripped apart Nos 119-121 Kingston by-pass. The three houses were demolished.

An oil bomb dropped on No 4 Highfield Road causing damage.

In Parkside Crescent, off Elmbridge Avenue, an HE bomb dropped, causing damage to Nos 15 and 17. Then an HE bomb fell on No 66 Elmbridge Avenue, reducing Nos 64-68 to ruins.

There was further damage in Elmbridge Avenue when an HE device came down in the road between the junctions of Elgar Avenue and Beresford Avenue. Several houses needed repairing.

A short while later, another high explosive bomb struck No 155 Elgar Avenue. Nos 153-157 were reduced to rubble. A similar bomb wiped out Nos 123 & 125 Beresford Avenue. The front garden of Nos 118 and 120 provided a landing pad for another HE bomb. The two houses were badly damaged.

Another HE device blew apart Nos 10 and 12 Elmbridge Avenue while nearby, along the meadows by the River Hogsmill, seven more HE bombs went off but property was spared.

An unexploded bomb was reported at No 50 Elmbridge Avenue. It later went off but it only ruptured the earth around and the house was saved. Another unexploded bomb later went off at No 161 Elgar Avenue. Nos 159 and 161 were demolished while Nos 163 and 165 suffered severe structural damage.

A V1 flying bomb — doodlebug, exploded on 23rd June 1944, at Nos 191 & 193 Ewell Road, Surbiton. Mrs Sylvia Roberts, 52; Cecil Evans, 35; and John Roberts, 50; all of No 191 were killed.

Also in Elmbridge Avenue the same day, a garage and coal bunker were burnt out at No 23.

On the Kingston bypass, Nos 170 and 174 had to be demolished after an HE bomb went off. The back of No 6 Oakdene Drive was hit and the blast damaged Nos 2-12.

A bomb also dropped on the garage of No 138 Kingston bypass causing damage. Yet another high explosive bomb fell on the ground of the Egmont Nursery but fortunately no damage occurred and no one was hurt. At the rear of No 73 Southwood Drive, an HE bomb also dropped but no damage was caused.

There were many other HE bombs that day. One descended on Nos 37 & 39 Collingwood Avenue and the back of the properties was badly affected by the blast.

A high explosive device fell on the front garden of No 45 Oakdene Drive, but no damage was reported.

An HE bomb then demolished Nos 29 & 33 Knollmead. Air raid wardens then heard of another device at the railway embankment causing slight damage to nearby properties.

Another three HE bombs were dropped in fields south of the railway embankment but no damage was reported.

Six houses were destroyed at Warren Drive when a high explosive bomb blasted apart Nos 153-163.

The grounds of Egmont Nursery suffered a hit again. Greenhouses were shattered when an unexploded bomb detonated. Another UXB was reported in the back garden No 50 Oakdene Drive but no damage was observed.

The blast from a UXB outside No 44 Knollmead resulted in its demolition and neighbouring houses needed repairing. An oil bomb struck No 5 Oakdene Drive, causing damage, but a similar device which hit the rear of No 23 Southwood Drive left the home unscathed.

An enemy plane, a Messerschmitt, crashed at the Maori Sports Ground, near Tolworth, the same day, killing its young crew of three.

On **12th September 1940**, an anti-aircraft bomb exploded under the driveway of No 92 Ditton Road without serious consequences. Three days later, on **15th September**, sheds were demolished behind No 35 Broomfield Road as a result of a high explosive bomb and another, which dropped outside the front of No 37, left Nos 35-39 needing extensive structural repairs. Yet another, in the garden of No 40, went off with minimal affect.

In Princes Avenue, an HE fell in the road by No 34. Fronts of adjoining houses were damaged. Another dropped in the road by No 20 Princes Avenue. The mains and the fronts of nearby houses were ripped open but another HE in the back garden of No 37 Oakleigh Avenue had no notable impact while another HE, in the back garden of No 22 Hook Rise, caused damage to the house. The same day, an HE had been found to have gone off on allotments in Hamilton Avenue and on the Kingston bypass in Hook Rise, where property was damaged.

continued on page 62

First doodlebug's remains . . after killing three at Hook

Wreckage of the expended flying bomb outside Nos 10 & 12 Whitehall Crescent, Hook, on 17th June 1944.

THIS is the twisted fuselage of a deadly weapon after performing its dastardly task of causing death and destruction. Hitler's first doodlebug to fall in the Surbiton borough came down in Whitehall Crescent, Hook, at breakfast time on Saturday 17th June 1944. It wrecked several bungalows built just five years earlier in the former grounds of a large, early 19th century house called Whitehall.

So great was the blast, it was said that two children, who were to be orphaned, ended up on the roof of their home. Their parents, Caleb Turnham and his wife, Edith, both 30, of No 4, were crushed to death. Marian Sanford, 82, of No 2, also suffered the same fate. Many homes in Clayton Road were damaged. Some say the flying bomb came from the direction of the North Star, Hook, and brushed a tree which turned it towards Whitehall Crescent plunging to the ground with devastating consequences. Fred Thompson, then of 67 Rhodrons Avenue, saw it arrive from the direction of Chessington North Station.

Resident Ivor Wagner, living at Ilford in 2002, still possessed furniture scratched by flying debris following the blast.

Mrs Betty Thompson, then 16, and of No 384 Hook Road, heard the engine cut out and dived under the bedclothes as it then exploded, shattering windows and showering the bed with glass.

Houses in Clayton Road, Hook, shaken after the doodlebug exploded in nearby Whitehall Crescent on 17th June 1944. The tall evergreen tree, seen above the roofs, was still standing in 2002.

Pilotless planes raid Surbiton borough

Flying bombs wreak havoc

BY 1944 Surbiton became a quieter place as far as incessant bombing was concerned. In fact, the last two years had been much calmer, compared with 1941. Peace was shattered in February 1944 when incendiary bombs rained down on Berrylands.

Germany was losing the war. The liberation of Europe began with the D-Day landings on 6th June, and that would have been the end of Surbiton's share of the bombing, were it not for the arrival of Germany's secret weapon. Only seven days had passed since the allied armies had landed on Normandy's beaches, when the first flying bombs came over the Channel. Before five months had passed, 23 local people would lose their lives because of them.

The RAF spotters called it Diver. Its designation was Fieseler Fi 103.The public called it the buzz-bomb — a doodlebug. It was in effect, a first generation cruise missile — an unmanned air-breathing jet aircraft with an explosive warhead and a guidance and targeting device.

It was a flying bomb, known to its creators as Vergeltungswaffe I — or Vengeance Weapon No 1. Between 13th June 1944 and 29th March 1945, thousands of V1s, as they were called, would be launched against Britain, causing as many deaths.

continued from page 60

On 25th September 1940, a bomb fell in the gardens of Nos 98-100 Ellerton Road, but no damage occurred. However, the bomb disposal squad extracted a 1,000 kilo UXB at the site in November 1941.

More bombs fell on **28th September**. A high-explosive blast resulted in Nos 33-39 Vincent Avenue being reduced to rubble. A similar bomb rocked No 71. Two HEs fell in fields south of the railway while another damaged houses around No 16 Alpine Avenue. The same day, Nos 4 & 6 Oakleigh Avenue were demolished by an HE and another damaged the rear of No 37 Princes Avenue. A similar device damaged the rear of No 19 Oakleigh Avenue. Yet another HE badly damaged shops at the back of No 23 Oakleigh Avenue.

Air raid patrols noted that two HEs fell also on allotments off Red Lion Road, and another on No 97 Red Lion Road, resulting in the demolition of Nos 95, 97 & 99. An HE blast at No 23 Pyne Road wrecked Nos 23,25 & 27. There was considerable damage to the interior of Windsor Laundry, Lenelby Road from another HE.

Nos 6 and 8 Draycott Road were destroyed by another high explosive. Nearby, in Douglas Road, No 124 was demolished and another HE next door in the garden. No 17 Ravenscar Road suffered a direct hit and it, together with neighbouring homes at Nos 15 & 19 were destroyed. In Berrylands, the junction of The Roystons and Raeburn Avenue was struck by an HE bomb. There was only slight damage to property.

At Largewood Avenue, an HE fell on No 109, demolishing the house and nos 107 and 111. A similar bomb destroyed Nos 47-57 Alpine Avenue after falling on Nos 51 & 53.

On **10th October 1940**, more HE bombs fell; one in Cranbourne Avenue, the other at No 168 Hook Rise. Both caused only slight disruption. Garages at Nos 7 & 9 Collingwood Avenue were also hit.

Roof and ceiling fire damage was logged at No 17 Alexander Drive and No 21 Kings Drive, Berrylands, on **11th October** after two incendiary bombs. In the Ewell Road, fire bombs damaged the roofs of No 398 Ewell Road, No 1 Elgar Avenue, No 3 Princes Avenue and No 11 Princes Avenue. In Berrylands, incendiary bombs the same day hit the roofs of No 1 & 14 Regent Road, No 12 The Ridge, and No 11 Berrylands.

An UXB went off at No 7a Surbiton Hill Park on **12th October**. The house was demolished. An HE bomb also hit Tolworth Court Farmhouse, causing damage. The nearby Maori Sports Ground was also hit by a HE.

On **14th October**, a builders' yard by Berrylands Hotel was hit by an HE bomb, damaging nearby property. The following day, an HE bomb fell in the middle of Princes Avenue, outside No 6, but homes escaped damage. However, at the corner of Raeburn Avenue and Ewell Road, shops and houses were badly damaged by a high explosive device and at the corner of Beresford Avenue and Warren Drive, there was some damage to property. Pyne Road was again hit by HE bombs. Nos 5 & 7 were demolished and around the corner, near Nos 81-85 Red Lion Road, another bomb fell on open ground, damaging No 81. Two bombs also dropped on allotments off Red Lion Road.

On 17th October an HE bomb destroyed Nos 285, 287, 289 & 291 Hook Rise. An oil bomb fell at the rear of No 283 Hook Rise. Both an HE and an oil bomb failed to damage Tolworth Central School after coming down on the playing fields the same day.

Wreckage of a V1 bomb in Greenfield Avenue.

On **22nd October 1940** the canteens at both Mollarts and Parnells' factories and gas mains were damaged by two HE bombs. Another similar device fell at No 129 Hook Rise, trapping people in an Anderson shelter. Nos 129,131, & 133 were later demolished.

After a week's respite from hits, Tolworth was again a target on **28th October**. An incendiary bomb burnt the roof and a small bedroom at No 36 Largewood Avenue.

On **8th November 1940** HE bombs dropped on the railway line at the rear of Alpine Avenue. The line was damaged and train services were suspended. Others came down in fields at Stevens Farm.

Nine days later, Tolworth Isolation Hospital, Red Lion Road, received a strike from two high explosive bombs. One landed in the driveway, the other on wards which were considerably damaged. Surrounding property was also damaged. Incredibly, there were only two slight casualties.

On **23rd November**, an HE bomb exploded in the back garden of No 12 Alpine Avenue. The back of No 52 Meadway was badly damaged and repairs were necessary on surrounding homes. A goods train was derailed on the line at the back of Alpine Avenue following the blast from another HE bomb. An unexploded bomb was also removed by the disposal squad from No 34 Alpine Avenue.

Seven days later, the blast from a HE on open ground at the rear of No 178 Elmbridge Avenue could be felt for miles around. Surrounding property needed repairing. The same day, an HE bomb fell in a field at the rear of the Mollart factory. A separate HE bomb which hit the allotments by No 168 Hook Rise demolished a garage.

9th December 1940: HE, in road opposite 7 Park Road — slight damage to property. UXB, in garden rear of No 28 Park Road. Removed by bomb disposal squad.

The bombing campaign was renewed in **January 1941**. On 11th, the rear of Nos 2 & 4 Chiltern Drive was struck, resulting in both properties being demolished. No 6 also suffered extensive damage. Nearby properties were also affected.

On **15th March 1941**, a high explosive device went off on the Red Lion allotments but there was no significant damage. Four days later a devastating bomb shattered the peace in Ravenscar Road. The HE device ripped apart Nos 22 & 24 and partly demolished Nos 26 & 28. Another HE bomb in the same street hit the front of No 19. The result was the demolition of Nos 19, 21, 23 & 25 Ravenscar Road. In addition, another HE bomb caused slight damage to No 45 while a similar device caused slight disruption at No 12.

An incendiary bomb set fire to the roof of No 132 Tolworth Road on **19th March**.

On **10th May 1940**, HE bombs dropped at Fishponds, Hollyfield Road , and on open ground nearby. Damage was slight. School shelters at Hollyfield Road escaped damage in another HE device that day.

Douglas Road, Tolworth, was in the firing line in the next spate of HE bombing on **28th July 1941**. A device fell at the rear of No 70, causing blast damage to neighbouring homes. Then, two other bombs hit both Nos 66 & 54. Both were reduced to rubble. The rear of No 50 was damaged by another HE blast. Next door, at No 48, was hit by another bomb and was demolished. Another four houses in the road, including Nos 15, 18 & 36, needed repairing after HE bombs exploded on footpaths. Nos 7,9, 11, 30 & 32 were pulled down after suffering direct hits from another two HE bombs. No 13 was partly demolished. A blast rocked the junction of Ewell Road and Douglas Road the same day, causing further damage and a separate bomb resulted in Nos 302, 304 & 306 Ewell Road being pulled down. A small British anti-personnel bomb was found in the debris at No 32. It did not go off.

On **3rd March 1943**, a shell exploded in Greenfield Avenue, causing slight damage to the roadway. A UX shell was found in **March 1943** at No 392a Ewell Road. The same day a garage was demolished by a shell falling at No 187 Elgar Avenue. An unexploded shell was then discovered at No 132 Warren Drive, in the garden and another in the back garden of No 1 Endway. Incendiary containers with considerable potential were dropped on No 11 Seymour Gardens and No 16 The Ridge, Berrylands. A shell went off in the Lagoon Passage, Berrylands, on **30th October 1943** and Surbiton Lagoon itself was slightly damaged on **6th February 1944** when an anti-aircraft shell exploded.

Some 580 incendiary bombs rained down on Berrylands on **23rd-24th February 1944**. Thirty-seven started damaging fires. Properties affected by IBs in that vigorous raid included No 22 Rose Walk, Nos 106, 108 & 138 Surbiton Hill Park, No 123 Chiltern Drive, No 39 The Roystons Nos 96, 111, 115, 89, 83, 78, 66, 58, 48, & 56 Berrylands, Nos 1 & 7 The Byeways, No 8 The Crest, No 37, 47 & 61 The Ridings, No 26 The Ridge, No 40 & 49 Berrylands Road, No 15 Manor Crescent, No 9 The Avenue, (Convent), No 106 Surbiton Hill Park, No 11 Seymour Gardens, No 99 Chiltern Drive, No 79 Berrylands, No 87 Berrylands, Regent Road Works, H C Jones and Co Ltd, Berrylands Station Booking Office and No 5 Berrylands. UXBS were found readily on the Alexandra Recreation Ground. Among them were four 500kg devices and three 50 kg bombs. There were no casualties or damage there. An incendiary bomb went off in Bond Road causing damage at Nos 70 & 74. UXBS were buried at No 81 Bond Road, No 116 Thornhill Road, and in Middletons laundry field near Tolworth Road. HE bombs went off at No 25 & 27 Fullers Avenue slightly damaging sheds. A UXB was buried at No 88 Tolworth Road and a fire bomb was also located. An unexploded anti-aircraft bomb was located on waste ground near No 24 Rose Walk and a UXB was reported at No 4 Thornhill Road.

'A motorbike engine' in the sky

V1 Tolworth tragedies

BY MIDDAY on June 16, 244 V1s had been launched from sites in the German-occupied Pas de Calais area. More than half of these crossed the Channel, and at first they were mistaken for German aircraft that had been hit, as the jet of flame looked like an engine on fire.

The noise of a V1 was unforgettable and many said it sounded similar to a motorbike engine that raced across the sky.

Flying at a constant height and on a straight course, the missile had a range of up to 150 miles and carried a warhead of more than 1,800lbs of amatol.This was sometimes supplemented with incendiary bombs.The fusing system was remarkably efficient and only four of the first 2,700 to fall had failed to detonate.

On 17th June, the first two V1s came down in the Surbiton borough. Four homes in Whitehall Crescent, Hook, were blown apart, killing three residents and causing extensive damage along Clayton Road, Hereford Way and Hook Road.

Within hours, the next flying bomb descended on Tolworth Park Road, bringing death and destruction. Twelve people died in the horrific attack from the blast and falling masonry.

There was much damage to houses in surrounding roads also.The bomb had produced a surface blast from a ton of high explosive.

Within the next few days, more doodlebugs would fall in the Surbiton borough.The tennis court by the lagoon at Berrylands was hit on 22nd June 1944, but no one was seriously hurt.The next day, three more V1s fell on the outskirts of Chessington, but the fourth came down on Nos 191-193 Ewell Road, near the Fishponds, killing three. Two more V1s descended on Chessington in early July, injuring residents and causing much damage.And on July 5, a resident of Elmbridge Avenue was killed.

Alfred Wall, aged 37, was killed on 5th July 1944 when a flying bomb dropped on Elmbridge Avenue (right). Nos 78, 80 & 82 were brought crashing down in the terrific explosion which followed.

ARP warden Jabez Summers and his wife Mary of No 6 Ashcombe Avenue died afer a flying bomb exploded at No 2 on 15th November 1944.

Surbiton evacuates 9,000 as buzz-bombs pose a peril

Flying bombs claim more lives

THE month of July 1944 also saw another large-scale evacuation of children and accompanying parents in the South East.

Memories of the Blitz were re-kindled when more than 1.5 million youngsters and adults were evacuated from London in a week.

Over 9,000 individuals left the Surbiton area to get away from the menace of the doodlebugs.

On 19th July, a V1 landed in the grounds of Chessington Zoo but fortunately no-one was killed. More injuries were sustained in Avenue South on 28th July when another destroyed three houses. Further casualties were found in the rubble of houses in Balaclava Road, where St Andrew's Hall was demolished. Incredibly, they did not lose their lives.

More than 100 launch sites were being used in France and Belgium for these terrifying inventions. They came by day and night with no human enemy to shoot down but the war against the V1 was being won, however.

Close proximity fuses were now used in gun shells which exploded within range of the target, which turned a near-miss of a V1 into a hit. This, along with a new radar system that plotted the course of the weapons, meant that by the end of August only one in seven of them got through to London and the suburbs.

By the end of August, the launch sites in the Pas de Calais region were closed down as the allies were closing in. The flying bombs were then launched instead from Holland.

Two more flying bombs would land in Surbiton. The first fell on Derby Road, Tolworth, on 5th October, destroying three homes and killing two people — Emma Barrie, aged 70, of No 14, and Cyril Kibble, aged 41, a visitor to No 17.

The second and last V1 in the Surbiton borough demolished a house in Ashcombe Avenue on 15th November, killing an air raid warden, Jabez Summers, aged 63, and his wife, Mary, 65.

More V1s would fall elsewhere but Surbiton's ordeal was over.

At the end of the war, it was estimated that over 9,000 V1s had been launched against London and 6,725 had reached England of which 2,340 had fallen in the greater London area.

More than 6,000 people were killed nationally and 18,000 injured by this awful invention.

The doodlebug's devastation in Derby Road, Tolworth, on 5th October 1944.

St Andrew's Hall and neighbouring houses were wrecked.

Another view of the destruction in Avenue South.

Top hat untouched in Avenue South blast

THREE houses were demolished by a flying bomb at Avenue South on 28th July 1944 and several people were injured and conveyed to hospital. Mrs Ernest Hopkins of No 18 had just enough time to get into her Morrison shelter with her dog before her house collapsed. In a very short time, she and the dog were extricated, and although, shaken, were uninjured. Amid the debris of a nearby destroyed house, one object lay intact — a top hat of Edwardian vintage. Close beside it was an untorn music sheet, blown, probably from a piano. It bore the title "Say It Isn't So", by Irving Berlin.

Three houses were demolished when a V1 "buzz-bomb" fell at Avenue South on 28th July 1944, injuring several people.

Three killed at zoo, Copt Gilders homes hit

Chessington tragedy

ON 2nd OCTOBER 1940, a high-explosive bomb fell on a shelter trench in Chessington Zoo at 4.40 in the morning, killing three people. The 55-year-old wife of keeper, Ernest George Arnold, of The Lodge, Chessington Zoo, lost her life, along with Ronnie Page, aged 10, and Mrs Annie Page, both of the Cottage, Chessington Zoo.

Other bombs blew off an ostrich's leg and destroyed a monkey cage and a penguin enclosure. A polar bear was said to have been scorched but unfazed by the experience.

Much damage in Chessington occurred at the newly-built Compton Crescent, Hemsby Road and Wilson Road.

On **1st July 1944**, a V1 doodlebug dived over the housing estate built on the former Copt Gilders Farm. It exploded on impact with the rear of No 28 Wilson Road, blowing up several houses in the neighbourhood.

At No 26 Wilson Road lived the Lloyd family.

Many years later, Ray, who was only one year old at the time, recalled the events as related to him by his parents.

"I was born at the house on **3rd May 1943** and my sister, Rita, five years earlier, in 1938. We lived on the end of a block of four. When my sister and I later saw the photo of the damage in *Chessington Remembered* we started to learn what our parents must have gone through when they came back to their damaged home from emergency housing in Ellerton Road.

"Although my dear dad was in the house when the doodlebug fell, how he was not killed will remain a mystery forever. He arrived down here in Worthing at our gran's house where Mum had brought my sister and me when the bombing got so bad. Dad arrived in just a pair of shoes, trousers and a mac someone had loaned him. It must have broken Mum's heart when she saw him, simply because she must have realised that our home had gone.

"My mum believed that so many homes were damaged or lost in this area because the Germans realised that by following the Kingston bypass, it would lead them to their ultimate and most wanted target — London. Therefore, my mum told me that the Germans called this road 'Dornier bypass'."

Five-year-old David Tippett-Wilson, was sitting eating egg on toast in the kitchen of his parents' home at No 159 Compton Crescent when the bomb went off.

He recalled: "We lost our roof. It was blown off in the blast. We had to move out."

The Wilson Road and Marston Avenue neighbourhood of Chessington after a doodlebug dived down on 1st July 1944. It exploded at the rear of Wilson Road causing much damage and injuring some householders trapped by falling masonry.

In the war years, families cheered each other up by putting on little shows on a small makeshift stage in Compton Crescent. The entertainment proved great fun for the children. David won a prize for his Royal Marines' costume.

The first recorded high-explosive bomb to drop in Chessington was on **27th August 1940** at No 2 Oak Cottages, almost opposite Byhurst Farm, Leatherhead Road. Much damage occurred. Another high-explosive bomb dropped in a field north of Rushett Farm on the same day.

On **9th September** the same year, a high-explosive bomb fell at the rear of Park Cottages, south of the lane to Barwell Court Farm, but there was no damage here or at the Sir Francis Barker recreation ground from a similar device. The same day an unexploded bomb was reported at the same playing field.

On **27th September 1940**, four HE bombs came down but failed to cause damage at the Bonesgate Brickfields, Moor Lane, but windows were cracked when two HE devices detonated at the Sir Francis Barker field.The next day, The Cottage in Cox Lane was destroyed when it took a direct hit from an incendiary bomb. On **30th September**, a HE bomb fell near the zoo but there was no damage caused.

An unexploded bomb was reported by wardens two days later on the railway between Chessington South and North Stations and in the front garden of 46 Stokesby Road and in the back garden of No 9 — the same day as the zoo fatalities — but there was no damage. Seven HE bombs dropped on Bunkers Hill, Leatherhead Road, again failing to cause interruption. On **4th October 1940** , two UXBs were discovered in fields at Rushett Lane, a HE went off and another bomb was reported.There was no damage.

On **7th October**, a UXB was logged in the Leatherhead Road between Fairoak Lane and the Fox and Hounds as were two HE bombs in the same locality.Two other types of bomb fell here, too. Four days later, a device dropped in woods behind Gilders Road and an UXB was also removed.

An HE bomb blew a large crater in Leatherhead Road, 300 yards north of The Star on **October 11th**, while a UXB was taken away from a footpath near St Mary's Church.

On **12th October**, there was slight damage to property when a bomb dropped on the Old Brightonians Recreation Ground. Two others dropped north of Chessington Zoo's driveway, both exploding. The next day, a HE bomb detonated in a field north of Roebuck Road.

Five days later, a bomb exploded in the tapir pen at the zoo, but there was no damage. Three HE bombs rocked the zoo vicinity and another HE went off on the railway embankment near the warden post at Chessington South.

Wardens based next to the Fairoak Brickyard reported that on **19th October 1940**, two HE bombs exploded in fields west of Barwell Court, as well as another device.

Three days later, an HE bomb went off between the warden's post and trenches in Gilders Road, but there was no damage. On this day, the bomb fell on Nos 13 and 15 Hemsby Road, leading to Nos 9,11,13 & 15 being demolished.

Additionally, two HE bombs and another device descended into fields at the rear of Gilders Road. Other HE bombs were reported 150 yards west of Leatherhead Road near Barwell and in fields at Byhurst Farm and 150 yards from Rushett Cottages.

On **25th October**, a bomb caused slight damage to property north of Barwell Court while two others came down in a field next to the Sir Francis Barker Recreation ground.

Part of the remains of Nos 9, 11, 13 &15 Hemsby Road, Chessington. These houses were only 10 years old when they took a direct hit from a German bomb on 22nd October 1940.

Two HE bombs and another device went off in Acre Field, and two HE bombs exploded in a field north of Barwell Court Drive. Two HE bombs also fell in a field south of Gilders Road and Billockby Close. Next day, another HE bomb descended at the rear of No 28 Roebuck Road.

On **6th November 1940** three HE bombs were registered in fields north of Gilders Road and Billockby Close and two days later, three HE bombs were logged in fields south west of Byhurst Farm. On 12th November, Leatherhead Road, 300 yards south of the zoo was partly blocked after another cluster of HE bombs fell.

Homes in Compton Crescent, Chessington, left in tatters after the flyng bomb blast of July 4th 1944.

Sisters among the 12 dead in Tolworth Park Road

Homes reduced to rubble at Tolworth Park Road after the V1 bomb fell on June 17th 1944.

TWELVE people were killed when a flying bomb dropped on Tolworth Park Road on Derby Day, Saturday 17th June 1944. Among those who lost their lives were two sisters, Barbara Gale, aged 21, and Brenda, just 12 years old. They lived at No 69.

The two girls were known to Raymond Hart, then of No 68 Largewood Avenue, Tolworth.

In retirement at Ash, near Aldershot, Mr Hart recalled: "At school and at play, I had got to know the Gale family of Tolworth Park Road. Among other things, two brothers, Des and 'Pip' Gale taught me to be a good butcher's boy.

"We worked for Messrs Baker and Blackwell on Saturdays. Their shop used to be at the lower end of Thornhill Road and we each earned the princely sum of 2/- for delivering meat on a Saturday morning. Sometimes these Saturdays were freezing cold and Des and Pip used to take me into their home in Tolworth Park Road for a cup of cocoa. Sadly that home was later hit by a V1 and we were all much saddened by the loss of two lovely sisters."

Other victims included Catherine Day, a policeman's wife, along with their son, Norman. A daughter, Katheen, survived.

It has also been suggested that a 13th casualty later died.

For local children, it wasn't just the loss of their dear friends which grieved them.

Mr Hart said: "My final living sadness of this nasty side of Tolworth at war was the fact that 'they' had hit Trickey's, at the corner of Ewell and Douglas Road. Trickey's was a wonderful toy shop that always had model trains running round its windows, especially at Christmas. All the boys always gathered there to watch and now it was gone forever. How could they do that to us?"

Mr Hart believes that the enemy had bombed Tolworth so heavily because of its armament factories.

"They were everywhere. Scattered along the Kingston bypass were Siebe Gorman, Parnall Aircraft, Nash and Thompson and many others sometimes disguised.

"Who remembers Fox and Nicholls on the Toby Jug corner doing other things than being a garage? And up Surbiton Hill, there used to be a garage called Plough Motors. They did not always do things with motor cars — perhaps they can proudly tell you that they once had admiralty contracts for doing things for submarines. And at the southern end of the old Ewell Road, there used to be a factory called Transceivers. In the war they made electronic communications equipment."

Queen Elizabeth, the future Queen Mother, tours the RAF base during her visit to Hook in 1939. A barrage balloon hangs above.

American Ambassador and PM Neville Chamberlain see war secrets at RAF base

King and Queen visit Hook Balloon Barrage Station

Queen Elizabeth (the future Queen Mother) surveys defence equipment at RAF Hook, on 16th April 1939. On the far right, Prime Minister Neville Chamberlain chats with RAF personnel. at the base in Mansfield Road.

US Ambassador Joseph Kennedy, with Prime Minister Neville Chamberlain at RAF Hook.

RAF Chessington started its life as RAF Hook Balloon Barrage Station in 1938 – the year before the outbreak of the Second World War.

A 45-acre site on the Chessington side of Mansfield Road, Hook, was used to build the base in the year Chamberlain signed the Munich Agreement with Hitler. The fields were part of the vast Lovelace estate when it was purchased by the Air Ministry in October 1937 to form one of 10 barrage balloon centres in and around London.

The site was to have 50 balloons from which dangled steel cables from a height of 25,000ft to stop raiding aircraft approaching at low altitudes.

Recruitment began in May 1938 for the two Territorial Air Service squadrons, 904 and 905, to be stationed at Hook as part of the Auxiliary Air Force rather than the regular RAF.

Building work on hangars began in the spring of 1938 and the RAF officially took over in the August.

The importance of the low profile station was suddenly magnified after a surprise visit by VIPs on 16th April 1939. King George VI and Queen Elizabeth (who became the Queen Mother), together with Prime Minister Neville Chamberlain and the US Ambassador, Joseph Kennedy (father of J F Kennedy), toured the site. The dignitaries had driven from Windsor for the visit.

Crowds lined the Hook Road to welcome the royal visitors to Hook. "Many cottages and houses were gaily decorated with flags and bunting and thousands of people thronged the roads to get a glimpse of the royal party," reported the Surrey Comet.

Some 1,200 auxiliaries and 200 regular RAF men were on parade for the occasion at which closely guarded barrage secrets were revealed to the special guests. Celia Collins, the young daughter of Mr and Mrs L Collins, of Hemsby Road, unsuccessfully tried to hand the Queen a bouquet.

he King and Queen inspecting a purity meter used for testing gas befo
the barrage balloons are inflated.

King Sees War Secret, Others Wait Outside

THE King and Queen had their first view of one of the recentl formed balloon-barrage squadrons yesterday when they motore rom Windsor Castle to Hook, on the outskirts of Surbiton.

They were accompanied by the Prime Minister and Mrs. Chamberlain, th merican Ambassador and Mrs. Kennedy, Princess Helena Victoria and othe the week-end guests at the castle. They stayed more than an hour.

National news: The King and Queen's visit to Hook.

Doodlebug's devastation in Derby Road leaves fiance dead

FLYING BOMB KILLS TWO

GIRL'S RESOURCE FREES FAMILY

CLOCK FOUND IN TREE

When a flying bomb fell in Southern England on Thursday, the enemy's wild and unfounded tales of the panic these visitations are supposed to cause were given the lie by a 15-years-old girl.

Mrs Ayliffe, with her mother and two children, Pamela and Joyce, were in the garden in their Anderson shelter, which, although intact after the explosion, was buried deep in debris, with the entrance completely blocked.

This might have caused a certain amount of alarm, but Pamela took it upon herself to reassure the others, and also remembered that her father had always left a spanner in the shelter for use in such an emergency.

She hunted around in the gloom until at last she found the spanner, and eventually managed to unbolt the back of the shelter, where the depth of rubble was not so great. The four occupants then scrambled out, little the worse for their experience.

An American soldier, who had not before had a "close up" of a flying bomb incident, sought out Pamela to take her picture by her buried Anderson, with the idea of letting "some of those guys way back see what they are missing."

HOUSES DAMAGED

A number of houses were damaged by the blast. Fruit trees in a garden were festooned with bits and pieces of household goods. A mattress blown off a bed, hung in a tree top, and there were also children's dolls and pieces of clothing.

In another tree was a clock which had stopped at the time of the explosion, but otherwise looked intact. Mr McCormack, whose home was badly damaged, found in his garden, much dented, a silver cup he won in a golf match.

The local first aid and rescue parties were quickly on the scene and the N.F.S. were called to deal with a small fire.

There were two fatal casualties, Miss Barrie and Mr C.J.Kibble, whose fiancee, Miss Robinson, was among the injured.

How the Surrey Comet reported the Derby Road bomb in 1944.

Homes at Nos 16, 14 & 12 Derby Road, Tolworth after a huge explosion caused by a doodlebug coming down on 5th October 1944. Miss Emma Barrie, aged 70, of No 14 and Cyril Kibble, aged 41, who was visiting No 17, and was engaged to be married, were killed after being struck by falling debris.

In Memory Of Residents Killed By Enemy Action In The Surbiton Borough During The Second World War

A full list of those who lost their lives through enemy action can now be published. All the names had been entered in Surbiton Hospital's mortuary book and the details kept at the town clerk's office. The names and addresses and dates when the individuals died have been listed so we can honour their memory. Behind each name is a tragic story. With the help of photographs and anecdotes in this book, there is an opportunity to remember the 59 innocent victims killed in World War Two.

Date	Name	Address
SEPT 9 1940	ELIZABETH LOVERIDGE, 41	66 ELMBRIDGE AVE
SEPT 25 1940	BETTY RAYSON, 20	9 CRANES PARK
SEPT 27 1940	FRANK COLLINS, 34	6 BRAMLEY MAN'S, EWELL RD
SEPT 29 1940	ELIZABETH KEENE, 80	124 DOUGLAS RD
SEPT 29 1940	JENNIE OBERG, 45	109 LARGEWOOD AVE
SEPT 29 1940	GERTRUDE BINGOTT, 50	111 LARGEWOOD AVE
SEPT 29 1940	ELIZABETH DUNNAGE, 70	37 VINCENT AVE
SEPT 29 1940	DOROTHY DUNNAGE, 25	37 VINCENT AVE
SEPT 29 1940	KATHLEEN DWYER, 75	39 VINCENT AVE
OCT 2 1940	MRS E. ARNOLD, 55	LODGE, CHESSINGTON ZOO
OCT 2 1940	ANNIE PAGE, 35	COTTAGE, CHESSINGTON ZOO
OCT 2 1940	RONALD PAGE, 10	COTTAGE, CHESSINGTON ZOO
OCT 10 1940	EDA NEWMAN, 38	158 KING CHARLES RD
OCT 13 1940	THOMAS ORE, 70	13 EVERSLEY RD
OCT 13 1940	EMILY ALEXANDER, 65	13 EVERSLEY RD
OCT 13 1940	KATHLEEN ALEXANDER, 29	13 EVERSLEY RD
OCT 15 1940	BRENDA ADAMS, 23	77 BOND RD
OCT 25 1940	EDWARD ROBBINS, 42	11 ASHBY AVE
NOV 3 1940	FREDERICK WHITE, 62	12 GUILFORD VILLAS
NOV 11 1940	EDITH THOMPSON, 37	8 GORDON RD
DEC 27 1940	ELLEN BICKNELL, 30	16 VILLIERS CLOSE
DEC 27 1940	ETHEL NASH, 48	18 VILLIERS CLOSE
DEC 27 1940	DAVID SKELTON, 7	20 VILLIERS CLOSE
DEC 31 1940	ELLEN MARSH, 71	61 ADDISON GDNS
JAN 10 1941	ELSIE PREESE, 39	44 RONELEAN RD
JAN 31 1941	ALBERT HOOKINGS	192 DOUGLAS RD
MAR 19 1941	ELIZABETH BAIGENT, 41	24 RAVENSCAR RD
MAR 19 1941	BRENDA RISING, 4	26 RAVENSCAR RD
JULY 28 1941	ANNIE HURSTWAITE, 78	7 DOUGLAS RD
JULY 28 1941	VIOLET ARCHER, 41	9 DOUGLAS RD
JULY 28 1941	RONALD ARCHER, 9	9 DOUGLAS RD
JULY 28 1941	JEAN STRONG, 9	9 DOUGLAS RD
JULY 28 1941	BARBARA STRONG, 5	9 DOUGLAS RD
JULY 28 1941	EDITH TRICKEY, 51	304 EWELL RD
AUG 8 1941	GEORGE SWAIN, 63	STREATLEY, DOUGLAS RD
AUG 16 1941	WILLIAM ROGERS, 27	24 FAIRMEAD
JUNE 17 1944	MARIAN SANFORD, 82	2 WHITEHALL CRES, HOOK
JUNE 17 1944	CALEB TURNHAM, 30	4 WHITEHALL CRES, HOOK
JUNE 17 1944	EDITH TURNHAM, 30	4 WHITEHALL CRES, HOOK
JUNE 17 1944	WALTER SIBLEY, 83	61 TOLWORTH PARK RD
JUNE 17 1944	CATHERINE DAY, 39	63 TOLWORTH PARK RD
JUNE 17 1944	NORMAN DAY, 14	63 TOLWORTH PARK RD
JUNE 17 1944	MARY LEAK, 70	65 TOLWORTH PARK RD
JUNE 17 1944	DICK SCRIVENER, 32	65 TOLWORTH PARK RD
JUNE 17 1944	MARJORIE SCRIVENER, 32	65 TOLWORTH PARK RD
JUNE 17 1944	ANTHONY SCRIVENER, 5	65 TOLWORTH PARK RD
JUNE 17 1944	BRIAN SCRIVENER, 2	65 TOLWORTH PARK RD
JUNE 17 1944	JULIAN WOODHAMS, 68	67 TOLWORTH PARK RD
JUNE 17 1944	WINIFRED O'ROURKE, 23	67 TOLWORTH PARK RD
JUNE 17 1944	BARBARA GALE, 21	69 TOLWORTH PARK RD
JUNE 17 1944	BRENDA GALE, 12	69 TOLWORTH PARK RD
JUNE 23 1944	JOHN ROBERTS, 50	191 EWELL RD
JUNE 23 1944	SYLVIA ROBERTS, 52	191 EWELL RD
JUNE 23 1944	LEONARD EVANS, 35	191 EWELL RD
JULY 5 1944	ALFRED WALL, 37	80 ELMBRIDGE AVE
OCT 5 1944	EMMA BARRIE, 70	14 DERBY RD
OCT 5 1944	CYRIL KIBBLE, 41	17 DERBY RD (VISITOR)
NOV 15 1944	JABEZ SUMMERS, 63	6 ASHCOMBE AVE
NOV 15 1944	MARY SUMMERS, 65	6 ASHCOMBE AVE

People living in Knollmead, Tolworth, celebrate with a street party for VE Day in 1945. The estate had suffered badly in the war. With rationing still in force, Surbiton's housewives had to be resourceful. At 60 Villiers Avenue, Elsie Howell made pancakes for her daughters, Muriel and Doreen, from flour, dried egg powder and lemonade. And they tasted good.

Residents of Northcote Avenue, Berrylands, celebrated VE Day in 1945 with a street party. The girl in the foreground with the floral dress is Joyce Spires, who has provided her wartime memories for inclusion in this book. Her mother, Katie Spires, is on the extreme right.

A log of the bombs that fell in Hook

(Excluding Hook Rise, Cox Lane, and area north of Ace of Spades)

7th November 1940: HE bomb, in field east of Glen Road. No damage.
12th November 1940: HE bomb, in field north of Mansfield Road. No damage.
14th November 1940: UXB in field at the rear of Brockett, No 205 Hook Road (house that became HQ of the General and Municipal Workers' Union). Removed by bomb disposal squad.
UXB in garden of Southernhay (Enid Blyton house) a few yards from Hook Road. Removed by bomb disposal squad. Disruption to traffic. Hook Road closed and route 65 buses forced to use diversion down Kingston bypass into Woodstock Lane, Clayton Road, rejoining Hook Road near White Hart.
5th January 1941: UXB, open ground near 'Moya', Fullers Way (South). Removed by bomb disposal squad.
23rd/24th February 1944: UXB buried, open ground south west of Civil Defence depot, Hook (now Woodgate Avenue estate). Reported as a 250kg bomb but bomb disposal squad confirmed 50kg. No damage or casualties.
UXB buried, open ground opposite No 5 Newlands Way. Reported as 250kg HE, but bomb disposal squad confirmed 50kg. No damage or casualties.
UXB buried, back garden of No 430 Hook Road. Bomb disposal squad confirmed 50kg. No damage.
UXB buried, open ground behind No 57 Hartfield Road. Confirmed 50kg by bomb disposal squad. No damage.
17th June 1944: Flying bomb, Whitehall Crescent. Extensive damage in Clayton Road, Hook Road and Hartfield Road. Three killed.

The staff of Legal and General were evacuated to Chessington Zoo in 1940 for a year. The manager was in a large room where there were cages of songbirds. "An interview with him was not easy with the twittering and singing in the background". Once, during a fish lunch, in walked a band of "damp and smelly" penguins, which "nestled by our legs seeking titbits".

The building of community air raid shelters in the Alexandra Recreation Ground off King Charles Road.

Community air raid shelters

COMMUNITY trench shelters were constructed in the Air Raid Precautions districts in Surbiton. When the bombing raids were frequent, the shelters were heavily used by folk unable to reach safety at home or who felt safer there.

The shelter in Stirling Walk, by Surbiton Lagoon, was built to house 76 people but was used regularly by about 150.

Extra shelters were dug out at Cottage Grove, Surbiton, and in the grounds of Croylands, Upper Brighton Road. Anderson shelters, being half-submerged in a back garden, could, and did, flood in wet weather. The Surrey Comet reported on the "appalling conditions" in the shelters in January 1941, with over 400 flooded. As a result, 3,855 Morrison shelters were provided free of charge. These took the form of an iron box-frame structure when assembled in a front room or wherever, with metal grilles covering the sides of the frame for added protection.

● The community shelters were at: Claremont Gardens (for 375 people); Burney Avenue/Ferguson Avenue junction (50); Upper Brighton Road, just south of railway next to ARP post (50); Next to Surbiton fire station, Ewell Road (150); By tennis courts, Berrylands; By Surbiton Lagoon (76); Present site of Edith Gardens, by ARP post (75); NW corner of Alexandra Recreation Ground (680); SW corner of Alexandra Recreation Ground (300); Lenelby Road (157); Hook Rise North (100); King George's Recreation Ground, Jubilee Way (100); Kingston Road opposite Tolworth Station (100); Warren Drive South, near Elmdene (100); Hook Recreation Ground behind parish hall (300); Moor Lane, Chessington, near Bridge Road junction ARP post (78); by ARP post, Gilders Road, near Filby Road (112).

The residents of Douglas Road, who had suffered so much during the war, had particular reason to celebrate VE day in 1945.

On rations: Mothers use their coupons at Fitch & Dobson, Ewell Road, Tolworth, in 1940. Illustration by Doreen Conroy.

A quick peep back

I thought about crawling back through my mind
To see what recesses I could find
Where my childhood is hidden now far away,
Will I remember how it was to play
At hide-and-seek in a field of wheat,
Or be a child at mother's feet?

Snippets dart in on a helter skelter,
"Come go down the shelter".
I'd dress up warm in my knitted gown,
Take my mother's hand as we hurried down
While my sister Pam, being nine years old
Ran on ahead without being told.

Then the sirens, the rockets, but I felt no fear
Because I knew my parents were near.
I just remember it warm with candles glowing,
But how often I have no way of knowing.
My father worked hard making fighter planes,
While sometimes we travelled north till it was safe again.

One memory made me laugh out loud,
Of running to school feeling very proud
As I clutched a banana I'd received that day
From my sister Gwen posted far far away.
It was blackened and limp, but of the smell,
Friends gathered around so they could look as well.
We had oats and sugar instead of sweets
With toast and dripping just for a treat.
How hard for my parents it must have been
To eke out our rations and not look mean.
The war ended after six long years
In a mesmeric collage of noise, colour and laughing tears.

So when did my childhood end, now exactly when?
I think when the boys all turned to men.

JILL ADAMS

Jill Adams, nee Evans, was born on 26th June 1935 at 44 Vincent Avenue, on the Sunray estate at Tolworth.

About the authors

MARK DAVISON was brought up in Bramham Gardens, Hook, where long before he was born, the first doodlebug to crash in the old borough of Surbiton came down just 100 yards away in Whitehall Crescent.

As an 11-year-old at St Paul's School, Hook, he was intrigued to be told this revelation by his teacher, Fred Clark.

A love of regional journalism took Mark into a career in local newspapers after he left Rivermead School, Kingston.

He is currently community editor of the Surrey Mirror at Reigate.

His passion for local history has resulted in him either compiling 17 books, including Tolworth Remembered, Hook Remembered and Hook Remembered Again. In the latter, he revealed that the famous author Thomas Hardy once lived in Hook Road and Mark was the first to locate the exact house.

Mark is also keen on popular music and the weather. His publications include the Surrey Weather Book and Surrey in the Hurricane.

While not burning the midnight oil researching and writing his books, Mark spends his free time travelling, learning the Czech language and occasionally checking out Surrey's snug country pubs.

He now lives in Reigate.

PAUL ADAMS was brought up in Long Ditton and has a keen interest in the changing face of the Surbiton, Tolworth and Dittons area. He has a wealth of anecdotes to offer readers.

He was educated at St Mary's School, Long Ditton, and then Hinchley Wood School. He has been involved in cartography and education welfare work. He assisted with the compilation of the book Long Ditton Remembered and is a co-author of Tolworth Remembered.

Paul enjoys treading the boards in amateur dramatics when time permits.

Other books in the series

- Tolworth Remembered, by Mark Davison and Paul Adams, £9.95
- Hook Remembered Again, by Mark Davison, £9.95
- Chessington Remembered, by Mark Davison, £9.95
- Hook Remembered, by Mark Davison £9.95
- Long Ditton Remembered, by Mark Davison
- Surbiton Memories and More Tales of old Tolworth and Berrylands by Mark Davison £9.95

Also available:

- Surrey Weather Book — a Century of Storms, Floods and Freezes, by Mark Davison and Ian Currie, £12.95
- Hampshire and Isle of Wight Weather Book, by Mark Davison and Ian Currie, £9.95
- Surrey in the Sixties, by Mark Davison and Ian Currie, £12.95
- Surrey in the Seventies, by Mark Davison and Ian Currie, £12.95
- East Surrey Then and Now, by Mark Davison £5.95
- Surrey in the Hurricane/London's Hurricane (storm of 1987) by Mark Davison and Ian Currie, both @ £9.95
- Kingston Then and Now by Margaret Bellars (1977) £9.95
- The Story of Kingston by June Sampson (1972) £9.95

To order any of these titles, please add £1.50 for p&p and send a cheque to Mark Davison, North Bank, Smoke Lane, Reigate, Surrey RH2 7HJ. Telephone 01737 221215 for further details.